Berg Women's Series

GW01005375

General Editor: MIRIAM KOCHAN

Gertrude Bell   SUSAN GOODMAN
Mme de Staël   RENEE WINEGARTEN
Emily Dickinson   DONNA DICKENSON

Mme de Staël, from a pastel by Isabey

Mme de Staël

Renee Winegarten

BERG *Leamington Spa/Dover NH/Heidelberg*

© copyright Berg Publishers 1985

British Library Cataloguing in Publication Data

Winegarten, Renée.
  Mme. de Staël.—(Berg women's series)
  1. Authors, French—19th century—Biography
  I. Title
  848'.609   PQ2431Z/

ISBN 0 907582 87 7
     0 907582 74 5 (pbk)

Library of Congress Cataloging-in-Publication Data

Winegarten, Renée.
  Mme. de Staël.

  (Berg women's series)
  Bibliography: p.
  Includes index.
  1. Staël, Madame de (Anne-Louise-Germaine), 1766 –
1817.   2. France—Civilization—1789 – 1830.
3. Intellectuals—France—Biography.   4. Authors,
French—19th century—Biography.   I. Title.   II. Series.
DC146.S7W56   1985   944.04′092′4 [B]   85 – 13104
ISBN 0 – 907582 – 74 – 5 (pbk.)
ISBN 0 – 907582 – 87 – 7

Published in 1985 by **Berg Publishers Ltd**,
24 Binswood Avenue, Leamington Spa, CV32 5SQ, UK
51 Washington Street,
Dover, New Hampshire 03820, USA
Panoramastr. 118,
6900 Heidelberg, West Germany

Printed by Billing & Sons, Worcester

Contents

Illustrations

To Asher—Always

1 The World of Germaine de Staël

'The first female writer of this, perhaps of any age', said Lord Byron, speaking of Germaine de Staël in a note to his poem, 'The Bride of Abydos'. True, the world-weary aristocrat found her 'overwhelming' personality and her voluble discourse on matters of moment somewhat difficult to bear, and he could not always resist making fun of her in his brilliantly flippant way. But that did not prevent him from recognizing her preeminence and acknowledging with genuine admiration her rare qualities of mind and heart. To one of Byron's acquaintances, Henri Beyle (many years before — as Stendhal — he wrote *The Red and the Black*), she meant even more. Stendhal made no allusion to gender, calling her 'the chief talent of the age'. As for Benjamin Constant, liberal politician, political theorist and her long-time lover and companion, trying to describe her impact in his auto-biographical novel, *Cécile*, he nominated her 'the most famous person of our age through her writings and her conversation'. Her mind was 'the most comprehensive that ever belonged to any woman, and perhaps to any man . . .', added Constant.

Germaine de Staël stood poised at the crossing point between two centuries: the eighteenth and the nineteenth. There were few paths into the modern world where she did not penetrate with her restless curiosity, to illuminate, create or change. She left her mark on the evolution of the novel as a genre, and it was she who demonstrated how vital was the role of writers, of literature and literary criticism in the creation and survival of a free society. The problems then facing women, and notably the woman writer of exceptional talent, were naturally of special urgency to her. She was concerned, too, with the quest for a more just and humane society and the principles of decent government upon which it depended; and long before George Orwell, she probed the language of politics and its current abuses. For her, the history of culture, which she outlined, was important for understanding not only the past but the present. Her ceaseless spirit of enquiry led her to be associated with the foundation of the Liberal movement in France, and with the national liberation of Italy and Germany.

1

But she was involved with the rise of internationalism as well as that of nationalism. For she had a sense of Europe itself as a cultural entity, and she envisaged a world community of men and women of talent who were devoted to thought and the dissemination of truth at all costs. It is the range and diversity of her interests that remain impressive, together with her capacity for creative thinking in many diverse fields that have since become highly specialized. Even now, writers in these areas can find that she blazed the trail for them. Many of her insights, gained from wrestling with the problems of her time, still concern us today.

Moreover, Germaine de Staël was no mere theoretician, confining her activity to the study. She lived intensely through a number of the grim events that accompanied the revolutionary overthrow of the old regime in France. To some degree, also, she was able to influence, if only behind the scenes, men who actually wielded power. She knew her finest hour when, meanly persecuted by Napoleon, she became the first and the most outstanding 'dissident' to oppose his arbitrary rule, and an exemplary figure in her own right. It was she who believed freedom to be as necessary as the air we breathe, and who carried forward the banner of liberty that Byron described as 'torn, but flying'.

Anne Louise Germaine Necker was just eight years old when Louis XVI ascended the French throne in May 1774. He inherited the forms of the absolute monarchy established by his ancestor, Louis XIV, a system already beginning to totter by the time of the long-lived Sun King's death nearly sixty years before. Louis XIV's costly wars, and those of his successors, had severely depleted the treasury. French intervention on the side of the colonists in the American War of Independence, some three years after Louis XVI's accession to the throne, would reduce the coffers still further. It would also contribute to throw into relief the difference between the regime in France, rooted in privilege (and the abuse of privilege), and the new republic whose founding fathers proclaimed the inalienable right to life, liberty and the pursuit of happiness.

The bitter misery of the lower orders in France, depicted as living little better than brute beasts by a compassionate observer at the end of the seventeenth century, had not much improved.

2

France was still primarily an agricultural country: the industrial revolution about to transform her rival across the Channel would not touch the French for some years to come. The heavy burden of feudal taxes still fell upon those least able to bear it, the peasants, while the privileged orders, the aristocracy and the Catholic clergy, enjoyed exemption. Shortages due to bad harvests led to numerous peasant uprisings: the worst of these occurred in May 1775, on the first anniversary of Louis XVI's accession.

Popular enough at first, Louis XVI was ill-suited to deal with recurrent crises. After his martyrdom on the guillotine it became customary to stress his domestic virtues, at least in comparison with his licentious predecessors. The king's chief passion was hunting (a royal and aristocratic preserve). According to a gentleman from Virginia, Thomas Jefferson, then a diplomat accredited to the French Court, the king was likely to be found on the hunting field or in his cups, 'and signs whatever he is bid'. True, influence no longer rested in the hands of princes of the blood or royal mistresses, like Madame de Pompadour, as it did during the reign of his dissolute grandfather. Nevertheless, the sincere efforts of reforming ministers (whether drawn from the liberal-minded members of the aristocracy or from the rising bourgeoisie), were frequently frustrated by Queen Marie-Antoinette or by the court party anxious to preserve the existing order and its privileges.

In June 1777, when Germaine was eleven years old, her father, Jacques Necker, was appointed Director General of Finance, a post of central importance which he occupied for four years, and to which he was recalled in August 1788, almost a year before the outbreak of the French Revolution. Nothing reveals more clearly than the phenomenal career of Jacques Necker the ascent of the moneyed bourgeoisie during the eighteenth century, or presages so well the progress of the middle class of entrepreneurs, financiers or lawyers, not only during the revolutionary period but in the following age. He was a Swiss-born Protestant, a self-made man who, rising to high position in the Thélusson Bank of Paris, managed to amass a fortune through speculation of an unspecified kind. He acquired with immense wealth a reputation for probity and efficiency. This reputation, doubtless fostered largely by his own writings, had spread to the country at large, so that when he was dismissed as Director General of Finance in July

1789, there was a popular outcry for his recall. He returned to his post, after the fall of the Bastille, amid unprecedented scenes of adulation. But it was already far too late: there was certainly nothing that one man could possibly do to halt the impetus of events. Despite Necker's loyalty to the king, however, the die-hard royalists would always persist in regarding him as one of the principal architects of the Revolution.

Through her father's eminent position, Germaine as a girl had become well acquainted with the manners of the court, which resided outside the capital in the grandiose palace built at Versailles by Louis XIV to enhance his own glory. There, in a pavilion in the vast gardens, with their symmetrical bosky vistas over parterres and fountains, Marie-Antoinette played at shepherdess and milkmaid, while nobles cooled their heels in the palace antechambers, hoping that the monarch would notice them and accede to their petition for an honour or a place.

The girl was also familiar with Parisian high society, which occupied the great mansions in the Marais quarter or in the newer faubourg Saint-Germain. Paris was smaller then, the Champs-Elysées still forming part of the countryside. Within the city wall, with its great *barrières* or gate-houses where the hated customs tax on goods entering the capital was collected, tall houses lined the busy streets. The wealthier and middle classes lived on the lower floors, the poor in the attics. These badly-lit and malodorous thoroughfares, where carriages constantly rumbled, turned to mud whenever rain carried dirt and rubbish along the gutters.

This was the city that Germaine adored, not only for its theatres where she could hear the tragedies of Racine and Voltaire or the operas of Gluck, but also because of the exquisite pleasure afforded by Parisian society in the last years of the old regime. Indeed, she was never to forget the brilliance, the charm, the elegance and the dazzling wit of the well-born men and women she frequented as 'Necker's daughter'. Many of them remained her closest friends, and to them her loyalty never wavered. One who looked back on this world, after it had vanished for ever, declared that those who had not known it had never experienced the true delights of living.

Yet inevitably there was another side to this agreeable society that was far less attractive. This was the Paris of prostitutes, libertines and gamblers, licentiousness and gambling being two of the principal ruinous diversions of the day. It was not at all uncommon for a man of fashion to incur huge debts at the gaming-tables or through maintaining his mistress in luxury — debts from which he could scarcely extricate himself except by marriage to an heiress, whose fortune he then rapidly proceeded to consume.

There was, moreover, the distasteful element of condescension, or worse, towards inferiors; and, apart from the king, everyone was inferior to somebody else. Throughout the eighteenth century, the abuse of privilege by those who had merely taken the trouble to be born, as Beaumarchais's Figaro remarked sarcastically, was exposed to irony and ridicule by the leading writers of the day. Principal among these was Voltaire, who had once been beaten up on the orders of an aristocrat he had offended. Mlle Necker, at the age of twelve, was taken by her mother to visit the aged Voltaire shortly before his death. Germaine admired the sage of Ferney, but she did not warm to him. She always felt that he had gone too far and that, through his mockery of superstition and ecclesiastical abuses, he had ended by undermining religion itself.

As a Protestant, though, she could not possibly forget all that Voltaire had done to rehabilitate Jean Calas, the Protestant merchant of Toulouse (wrongly accused of having killed his own son to prevent him from becoming a Catholic), who died, broken on the wheel, four years before she was born. The savage persecution of the Protestants under Louis XIV, which led to their dispersion, had not been forgotten, since her mother's family had been obliged to join the exodus. She knew well enough the price her co-religionists had paid to uphold a faith that was always associated in her mind with freedom and free inquiry. When minister of finance, her father himself was at first denied a place on the king's council because he was a Protestant, and had been invited to change his religion. The same stupidity, bigotry and fanaticism that Voltaire fought throughout his life, with all the subtle weapons in his armoury, would remain the targets of her own wit.

Eminent figures in the struggle for religious toleration frequented her mother's Parisian salon, one of the most celebrated in the last years of the old regime. Many of these writers were associated with the *Encyclopédie*, the creation of Diderot and D'Alembert, that extraordinary undertaking intended not only as a compendium of all existing knowledge but as a new way of envisaging the world and reorganizing it. The watchword of these *philosophes* of the Enlightenment (or all-embracing intellectuals, as we should call them, a word that had not yet been invented) was liberty. Not all of them meant the same thing by it. For Voltaire, for instance, it implied some form of enlightened despotism. To Montesquieu, author of *The Spirit of the Laws*, a work Germaine profoundly admired and which influenced her own thinking, it signified liberalism under a constitutional monarchy on the English model. The English style of government served as a handy weapon with which to beat the French system and all that was unjust and backward in it. Admiration for almost everything English, current among the educated in eighteenth-century France, reached its height in the Anglomania of the end of the old regime, extending from ideas to fashions in dress. It was a trend in which Necker and his daughter participated: to them, England — notwithstanding the great power of the aristocracy — provided an example of the good and desirable society.

The writer who, with Montesquieu, had the most enduring effect on Germaine, was Jean-Jacques Rousseau, born like her father in Geneva. Many of the poets, scholars and writers to be found in her mother's salon were personally acquainted with this difficult, moody, bizarre and far-ranging original thinker who shattered the preconceptions of his contemporaries. From these men of letters she could have learned much about Jean-Jacques, though she never met him herself as a child (he died, like Voltaire, in 1778). Her first published writing was an essay on the author of *Emile*, an essay which made a considerable stir at the time. But the work of Rousseau's that most deeply affected her, as it did sensitive souls in her own and succeeding generations, was his novel, *La Nouvelle Héloïse*. This book fostered a new kind of sensibility, daring in its hostility to convention and in its exaltation of spontaneity and of the rights of passionate love. The impassioned vicissitudes of the high-minded Julie and the noble Saint-Preux would move to tears and arouse the emulation of those readers, men as well as women, who were to follow this ideal as ardently as they could in their own attitudes and lives.

From the complex movement of the Enlightenment in all its

rich variety, Germaine would derive her trust in the spirit of free inquiry and her love of the open mind; the thrill she felt in thinking for herself and making discoveries of her own; her faith in the supremacy of reason, by which she meant having sensible ideas about everything. She was brought up among *philosophes* who asked important questions, who discussed new possibilities with excitement. What new heights might not humanity achieve in a kingdom governed by reason and justice? This was the age when the attainment of such heights appeared eminently feasible, if only the right enlightened government and institutions could be found and solidly established. It was idealism of this kind which made some French noblemen contribute to the abolition of their own privileges.

The immense surge of optimism, however, was counterbalanced, sometimes within the same person, by feelings of pessimism about human nature, by a sense of the oppressive limitations of human existence. Together with high hopes of human advancement there could be found a kind of morbid melancholy, bred by religious fears. Germaine's mother, for instance, offered an extreme example of such morbidity in her anguish about bodily corruption. Her charitable work had taken her into hospitals where, to her horror, she came upon cases of sick people being buried before they were clinically dead. She wrote a treatise on premature burial, and was so obsessed by the dread of the same thing happening to herself that she spent years in the study of her funeral arrangements, leaving detailed instructions that her body was to be preserved in a marble bath of alcohol in a private mausoleum. These instructions were faithfully carried out by Necker, whose corpse would be similarly treated.

The melancholy strain was reinforced by the grisly turn taken by events after the fall of the Bastille. 'A la lanterne!' was the cry heard by the hated financier, Foullon, who had once rashly suggested that the starving populace should eat grass. The mob strung him up on the bracket of a street light, murdered his son-in-law, and paraded their severed heads on pikes. From the window of his room in the rue de Richelieu the horrified vicomte de Chateaubriand saw the assassins dancing and singing as they thrust the bloody heads towards him — Foullon's mouth being filled with grass. 'Wretches', cried Chateaubriand, unable to control his indignation, 'Is this what you mean by liberty?' Such ghastly episodes seemed at first to be a kind of aberration, which could not be allowed to mar the feeling of revolutionary euphoria.

Everything seemed possible, everything was being discussed in the early months of the Revolution. 'All over Paris', wrote Chateaubriand afterwards, evoking the year 1789/90, 'there were literary assemblies, political gatherings, theatrical performances . . . . People went from the Club des Feuillants to the Club des Jacobins, from balls and gambling dens to public meetings in the Palais-Royal, from the rostrum of the National Assembly to the rostrum in the open air.' But soon, for all those moderate reformers, intoxicated by the new freedom, who had dreamed of the constant progression to a better world that would foster a better life for all human beings, and who believed that they had found the formula to help bring about this longed-for future, there were shocks in store. They could not explain to themselves the rise of demagogues like Marat, of Danton and the Girondins, still less that of Robespierre, Saint-Just and the Jacobin party, who all went so much further than the moderates had intended. The massacres of September 1792, when prisoners were ruthlessly slaughtered; the execution of Louis XVI in January 1793; and above all, the Reign of Terror from June 1793 to July 1794, delivered a series of blows from which the liberal idealists never fully recovered.

The Terror consumed Danton and his friends who had voted for the king's death, and all those men and women, whether aristocrats or not, who were accused of being in league with the enemies of the people. The luckless victims filled the tumbrils that passed along the rue Saint-Honoré to the guillotine, set up in what is now the Place de la Concorde. In the provinces, there were senseless killings of unspeakable savagery. Hundreds of young peasants of both sexes were either shot or clubbed to death in Britanny. The aged, women with babies, boys and girls, were taken out in rafts into the middle of the river Loire and drowned. Men were tied together and mowed down outside the city of Lyons. All these insane crimes were committed in the name of liberty, equality, fraternity, or in that of patriotism, national security and revolutionary justice. How had this terrible reversal come about?

To some, the marquis de Sade, in his reflections published in the 1790s and in his dark accounts of lust and torture, might seem nearer the mark than the followers of Rousseau, proponents of the essential goodness of human nature corrupted by society. 'What mortal is fool enough to assert, against all the evidence, that men are born with equal rights or strength?' inquired the divine marquis. 'Only a misanthropist like Rousseau would dare to establish such a paradox, because being very weak himself, he prefers to degrade to his own level those to whom he did not dare raise himself.' When he wrote those words, Sade was thinking of recent revolutionary history. Germaine, too, would try to find some way of coping with the bitter facts of the Terror. It would haunt her for the rest of her life. Yet she would never agree with Sade or with another contemporary of hers, the devout and gloomy counter-revolutionary writer, Joseph de Maistre, who envisaged the world in terms of victims and executioners, subject to 'the universal law of the violent destruction of living beings'.

During the revolutionary upheaval, when the die-hard royalists joined with foreign powers to overthrow the new regime, and when Frenchman fought against Frenchman, political life in France took that turn towards civil war which has shadowed it ever since. A number of Germaine's friends or members of their family were hunted down, imprisoned, guillotined. Others, women as well as men, were forced to flee to the far corners of the earth: some took refuge across the Channel, the Rhine or the Elbe; some sought asylum across the Atlantic. At the same time, the victorious soldiers of the revolutionary armies of the new French Republic were carrying the Revolution and its ideas beyond France's frontiers and, under the Corsican military genius, Napoleon Bonaparte, were moving rapidly to Italy and Egypt, and eventually from Spain to Russia. The whole world was opening up to a great many people who previously would rarely have moved beyond their village and provincial capital, or from their country estate to Paris.

Moreover, now that aristocratic birth was no longer a prerequisite for high position in the army, the Church and elsewhere, men could rise by relying solely on their own talents. The astounding career of Bonaparte himself dazzled the imagination. All those who might have expected to live out their days under the constricting forms of a centuries-old monarchy, lurched into a Republic ruled by a ruthless Committee of Public Safety, and then, after the downfall of Robespierre in July 1794, into the regime known as the Directory, where executive authority was vested in five Directors. By this time, people were sated with the gruesome excesses of the Terror, and all that the survivors wanted was peace and quiet.

Instead, they witnessed a great upsurge of living for self and pleasure. This was an era of greedy contractors and speculators successfully on the make. It was, too, an era of influential salon hostesses, like the beautiful Creole, Joséphine, widow of General Beauharnais, mistress of the powerful Director, Paul-Jean Barras, and later mistress and wife of Bonaparte; or Thérèse Cabarrus (wife of the Director, Jean-Lambert Tallien), who created the fashion for revealing dresses in the 'Greek' style, in diaphanous muslin. To stay in power, the Directory promoted successive *coups d'état* aimed at frustrating the Jacobins on the one hand and the ultra-royalists on the other, whenever either of these parties seemed likely to win the elections. However, the *coup d'état* of 18 Brumaire (November) 1799, engineered by General Bonaparte and his brother Lucien, closed the series.

The metamorphoses of General Bonaparte, laurel-crowned hero of the revolutionary Republic, who became First Consul (1799), then Consul for Life (1802), and in a final apotheosis, Emperor (1804), presented certain difficulties for those who esteemed consistency of conduct and principle. He found thrones for members of his family, and granted high positions to former constitutional monarchists, Jacobins and royalists who profited by his personal centralized government. Many were content to submit to the formalities of his court, to join his newly-created Napoleonic nobility, or to serve in the bureaucracy required by his endless wars of self-aggrandizement. It suited him well to let others dispute whether he continued the Revolution or destroyed it.

It was a world of grandeur and glory, of brilliant uniforms. It was also a world of spying, corruption, abasement and survival through changing allegiance to rapidly succeeding regimes. The First Empire, which seemed impregnable, lasted ten years. With Napoleon's defeat by the European Coalition and his abdication in 1814, the brother of the martyred king ascended the throne as Louis XVIII, only to flee ignominiously when Napoleon escaped from the island of Elba and landed at Golfe Juan. Defeated at Waterloo in 1815 after a reign of a Hundred Days, Napoleon was imprisoned on the island of Saint Helena while the victorious

Allies once again installed Louis XVIII on the throne. So it was that Germaine ended her days during the Restoration of the Bourbons, under a monarch whom she had never greatly respected as a man, and under a regime which had granted a Constitutional Charter, but which was dominated by the obscurantist forces of political and religious reaction.

Germaine's rise to prominence as a woman writer of serious works on politics, ideas and literature as well as the author of two epoch-making novels — a woman seeking to influence the course of public affairs — was effected against enduring prejudice. Any woman who meddled in political matters — and it was usually seen as meddling — must necessarily be involved in intrigue. The only political role for a woman in the eighteenth century was that of the salon hostess who, like the ambitious Mme de Tencin, manoeuvred behind the scenes on behalf of her brother the Cardinal. Exception was made, of course, if the woman were a ruler like Catherine II of Russia, in which case nobody found her conduct to be against the natural order of things.

In this so-called natural order, the intellect was perceived as a masculine attribute well into the nineteenth century and beyond. A woman of high intellectual attainments was thus inevitably seen as masculine, and therefore unnatural. Consequently, even the most intelligent men could find something odd and extraordinary about her — indeed, Germaine was led to feel this herself. For Balzac, the creator of the *Comédie humaine*, such rare women are objects of curiosity, who need to be explained and justified; they are even 'monstrous apparitions'. His remarks on the 'monstrous' character of the woman of intellect or genius were written more than two decades after Germaine's death.

A well-born girl's education in the eighteenth century, and after, was all too commonly limited to social accomplishments like music, sketching and dancing, in addition to a little suitable reading of poetical, moral or devout works. Only those girls whose fathers were large-minded scholars and savants, or who found the opportunity to look into their brothers' books, managed to acquire some learning. Germaine's education was quite exceptional because it was undertaken by her mother, the daughter of a learned Swiss pastor, and noted in her own right for her knowledge of Latin, and even a little Greek, as well as geometry and physics. It was exceptional, too, because as a child Germaine was allowed to associate with the eminent figures of the Enlightenment who were to be found in her mother's salon.

She was more fortunate in this regard, and as a Protestant, than most girls of good family in France, who were educated from a very early age in the convent. It was customary for French girls to leave the convent by the time they were sixteen, when they were quickly married off to a man usually considerably older than themselves, selected by their parents. Marriage was a matter of property and position rather than inclination. Therefore it was not considered in the least surprising in Parisian society if the marriage were a mere social façade, the husband taking a mistress and the wife a lover, so long as all was performed with perfect discretion, and above all, so long as there was no hint of scandal. Should any scandal arise, it was the wife, not the husband, who suffered and was ostracized.

This double standard was, and continued to be, a notorious injustice, criticized by enlightened men themselves. 'French public opinion frightened me', observed the narrator in the Swiss-born Benjamin Constant's novel, *Cécile*, 'this kind of public opinion which pardons every vice, but is inexorable on social conventions . . .'. In the 1790s General d'Arblay, a French *émigré* in England, trying to explain the customs of his native land to the novelist Fanny Burney, his future wife, told her: 'Our manners, in several ways, are so little in accord with those of this country, . . . that truly it would be not only unfair but cruel to seek therein the bases for one's judgment — our marriages, for instance. All of them were, so to speak, nothing but more or less painful sacrifices to social conventions, where the women have always been the victims, above all in the class of society which so far occupies the loftiest position.' The social conventions in France could present a severe handicap to any woman seeking to follow the example of full and free self-expression set by Rousseau for himself.

Despite this attitude to marriage, especially among the upper reaches of society, Germaine felt that there existed a greater concentration upon domestic virtues in the last years of the eighteenth century. These virtues were relative and were presumably to be found chiefly among members of the bourgeoisie, like her own parents. While motherhood in the abstract was idealized, in practice a more casual attitude prevailed. Around the middle of the century, the idea that a lady should breast-feed her own infant — instead of handing the baby to some young peasant woman who had just given birth — began to gain ground. The custom of passing the new-born baby to a wet-nurse persisted, however, well into the nineteenth century. It was doubtless one cause of the high infant mortality rate.

As for unwanted babies born of irregular unions, these were simply placed in the foundling hospital or abandoned in the street. Jean-Jacques Rousseau, notwithstanding his concern for the fate of humanity, disposed of all his illegitimate offspring in the foundling hospital. As an infant, one of the most celebrated figures of the age, D'Alembert, had been deposited by his well-born mother, Mme de Tencin, in a basket at a church door, but had been discovered and educated at his father's expense. Perhaps some allowance has to be made for a sheltered woman's ignorance of physiological niceties in the eighteenth century. The well-read Mme Necker herself had no idea of what was involved in childbirth, so that what she called the 'revolting details' of giving birth to Germaine left her in a state of profound shock. When Germaine was married at the age of nineteen, she confessed to knowing nothing about sexual matters.

Whatever their disabilities, women were thought to be significantly influential in an unprecedented manner in the eighteenth century. One sphere for their talents lay in the realm of social charm, as exercised in the salon, an institution founded in the previous century, where it had served to refine the brutal manners of a society emerging from the wars of religion. According to the eminent critic, Sainte-Beuve, it was not enough to be rich, to have a good cook, a comfortable house in a good district, and a longing for society, in order to establish a salon in the real sense of the word. These would merely attract all and sundry for a brief fashionable moment. And it was not necessary to be well-born or particularly well educated. The vital qualities for the hostess were a ready wit which took the place of learning, a knowledge of character and conduct, and an ability to think and converse on all kinds of topics with a smile, in a light, elegant and entertaining way. In the great salons of the eighteenth century, men of letters mingled with men of rank, moving to different circles on different evenings of the week. Gradually, with the growing interest in political reform, the salons took a more political turn, Mme Necker's serving in some respects as a kind of propaganda-centre to support her husband's policies. But wit, grace and style remained essential prerequisites.

Another sphere in which the influence of women was increasing was that of literature. With greater leisure in the eighteenth century, women not only read novels, they took to writing them, in England, France and elsewhere. Indeed, women novelists, like Fanny Burney or Mme de Charrière, with their gift for keen observation of the nuances of conduct, were already recognized as leading exponents of the genre. Very many others, extremely popular and esteemed in their day, are now largely unread. On occasion, their books were published anonymously. Some, like Mme de Souza, would even take to writing novels as a pastime. Others, forced to emigrate during the Revolution and exposed to the problems of the wider world, felt impelled to write about their experiences, or were obliged to do so by economic necessity. Women writers might concern themselves with such themes as education and moral conduct, which they considered a properly feminine sphere of interest, but they did not tend to publish original works expressing general ideas, as Germaine was to do.

However, despite their increasing prominence as novelists, women were rarely encouraged to write or publish. It was not unusual for them to be made to feel that writing for the public was incompatible with their domestic role and duties. Prejudice against women as writers persisted. Necker himself, with literary ambitions of his own which he was able to fulfil, had no taste for women writers. He was annoyed to find his wife engaged in writing, and forbade her to do so: he did not want Mme Necker to be pursuing an idea when she was with him. Nor did he approve of his young daughter's writing either. In order to satisfy her father's caprice, Germaine never sat at a desk to write while he was alive, and adopted various subterfuges to prevent him from discovering her in the act of writing. One is reminded of Jane Austen (nine years her junior), hastily concealing her manuscript whenever anyone entered the room. But whereas Jane Austen once remarked, 'I think I may boast myself to be the most unlearned and uninformed female who ever dared to be an authoress', Germaine had no intention of making light of her intelligence. On the contrary, she was proud to display it.

The question of equal rights for women was raised during the French Revolution by the marquis de Condorcet, the *philosophe* who declared in 1790 that 'Either no member of the human race has real rights, or else all have the same . . .', and that included black slaves and women. The upheaval brought some women briefly near the political arena itself, in quest of equal rights. Following the *Declaration of the Rights of Man*, Olympe de Gouges published her *Declaration of the Rights of Woman and of the Citizeness* (1791). 'Woman, awake . . .', cried Olympe de Gouges. 'What have you gained from the Revolution?', she asked her sex. (She was to die by the guillotine.) In England in the following year, 1792, Mary Wollstonecraft (who had translated one of Necker's works into English) published *A Vindication of the Rights of Woman*, where she violently attacked Germaine's youthful acceptance of Rousseau's condescending attitude to women in his *Emile*: 'It is not empire, — but equality that they should strive for', proclaimed Mary Wollstonecraft, who went to live in Paris in 1793, a friend of leading Girondins like Mme Roland.

On the model of the men's revolutionary clubs, women founded clubs of their own, like the 'Women Friends of Truth', the 'Revolutionary Citizenesses', or the more extreme 'Society of Revolutionary Republican Women' whose members caused a stir by parading in red and white striped trousers. One young court-esan, Théroigne de Méricourt, could be seen, dressed in a riding habit, haranguing women in the street and claiming a role for them in the National Assembly. Unfortunately, in June 1793, she was attacked by some women opponents in the gardens of the Tuileries, stripped naked and stoned. Her wits were turned, and she had to spend the rest of her life in an asylum.

More celebrated than the luckless Théroigne de Méricourt and the ill-fated Olympe de Gouges, both plebeian in origin, were two women of higher social standing: Charlotte Corday, assassin of the demagogue Marat, and Manon Roland. It was through her husband and her lover, both leading Girondins, that Mme Roland exercised political influence. She once spoke of Germaine, querying some scurrilous rumour about her. With the fall of the Girondins, Mme Roland perished with her friends on the guillotine, uttering her celebrated cry, 'Liberty, what crimes are committed in your name!'. At her execution, she was denounced in the press as 'a monster', a mother who 'sacrificed nature in wanting to rise above herself . . .'. All the women who attracted public notice of any kind, whether they tried seriously to improve the condition of their sex or not, found themselves qualified as prostitutes.

Those women who, in the early years of the Revolution, shared high hopes of remedying the injustices to their sex, saw their hopes dashed by the puritanical Jacobins. Under Robespierre, the women's clubs were closed down. It was not until the Directory that women again rose to prominence, but then principally in their former role of important salon hostesses, not as activists struggling for political equality. As for Bonaparte, he disliked intellectuals in general and women intellectuals in particular. On his couch in his inner sanctum, in a few moments of pleasure snatched between affairs of state or war, that was where he wanted women who knew their place. He did not want to hear female voices raised about matters that, in his view, were not their concern. All the same, when Bonaparte told Mme de Condorcet (widow of the apostle of human perfectibility who had poisoned himself to escape the guillotine) that women should not meddle in politics, she was moved to retort: 'In a country where women get their heads cut off, it is natural that they should want to know the reason why'. This standpoint seemed eminently reasonable to Germaine.

Hers was at first an era of intellectual and political rather than literary and artistic ferment, though in the end the arts could not remain untouched. By the time of her début, the style of Versailles in the arts had spread to all the courts of Europe; French was the language of the cultivated person everywhere; and Paris the centre of the civilized world. In literature, the lofty decorum of great writers who flourished in the reign of Louis XIV, together with the guidelines established by seventeenth-century critics, had declined into a petty tyranny of rules for their successors in the eighteenth century, and were questioned or ignored by more daring spirits inside and outside France. But these standards of a former age still largely predominated in influential Parisian circles, despite the immense changes that were taking place in French society as a whole, during and after the Revolution.

It was during Germaine's lifetime, for instance, that the press began to acquire an unprecedented influence. Immediately before the Revolution, there were about sixty papers in the whole of France. By 1795 there were more than two hundred in Paris alone, usually quite small sheets published every few days. Press freedom often degenerated into licence, especially under the Directory, which occasionally pounced, placing editors under arrest or deporting journalists to French Guiana. By then, many people had acquired the taste for a free press, but Napoleon soon put an end to such liberties. Under the First Empire, officially-inspired journals not only furthered Napoleon's policies but also sustained the established French taste in literature, either out of chauvinism or for political reasons.

For all exponents of the arts under Napoleon were expected to sing his praises, as they had once sung those of Louis XIV. Great painters like David, the once notorious Jacobin, and Ingres would serve the Emperor's interests. David would depict the heroic Emperor still watchfully awake and at work in his study as his subjects slept; while Ingres was to represent Napoleon on the imperial throne in the pose of omnipotent Jupiter. The neo-classical style which had begun as a forceful reaction against the convolutions or the libertinism of rococo, eventually served as the official art, first of the Jacobins and then of Napoleon.

Originally, the neo-classical revival had offered a return to a noble simplicity. Sublime acts of stoic courage or magnanimity, great deeds that displayed singular devotion to duty and love of country, drawn particularly from Roman legend or history — these provided the inspiring themes in painting as in drama or *opera seria*. In the neo-classical mode, it was felt that art and literature should have a universal appeal suited to men of all periods, not just to the individual in his own day. The ideal of the 'sublime' vision predominated in high art; and sublimity entailed a certain degree of elimination or purification of the common details of ordinary existence.

This kind of ennobling sensibility, which governed beings pursued by a mysterious melancholy, haunted by suffering and death, exalted and destroyed by the ineluctable force of tragic passion, would be absorbed and transfigured by the early writers of the French Romantic movement. It was a sensibility shared by Germaine herself, and she was to play a very large and innovative part in the process of that transformation into something rich, strange and essentially modern.

17

2 Education of a Female Prodigy

Anne Louise Germaine Necker, affectionately known as Minette, was an only child. This meant that she was the centre of her devout mother's attention in her earliest years, for at first her father, busy with financial concerns and affairs of state, stood somewhat aloof. Perhaps secretly he would have preferred an heir. The girl would eventually try to prove herself worthy of him through her activity and her quest for fame. Moreover, she was the only child of parents who had risen from obscurity as foreigners to wealth and high position at the most exclusive and imitated court in Europe. None of the Neckers ever forgot that they were exceptional beings with an exceptional destiny.

That she was born of Swiss parents in Paris, on 22 April 1766, would vitally influence the course of her life. To her, it was always obvious that she was French by birth, the product of French culture, anxious to foster the well-being of her compatriots. To outsiders, she would always seem the embodiment of everything Gallic in taste and outlook. But to many of her French contemporaries she remained a person of Swiss origin who went on to marry a Swedish diplomat: a foreigner, in short. This attitude was to prove a pretext for many of her later misfortunes.

There is no doubt that her hothouse upbringing at the hands of her over-scrupulous mother was strange. But then there was nothing commonplace about Mme Necker and her tormented introspection. A young woman of good looks, considerable learning and ambition, Suzanne Curchod, as she then was, had attracted the attentions of the young Edward Gibbon, the future historian of the decline and fall of the Roman Empire, when he was staying in Switzerland. At the behest of his father, however, Gibbon had broken with her in a highly insensitive way. From this humiliation and her place as a governess and then as a lady's companion, to which she had been reduced by poverty at her father's death, she was rescued by Jacques Necker. It was her ambition to see that their daughter should become someone out of the ordinary who would be a credit to her teaching and worthy of all her efforts.

A woman of extremely passionate character, Mme Necker was a strict Calvinist who tried to restrain her own vehement, self-dramatizing nature. This self-control, together with the fact that she was partially deaf, gave her an air of stiffness and constraint. Her watchword was duty, and she carefully divided her day into her duty to God, her husband, her child, her friends, the poor, the household, her toilette. It was not long before she perceived that her Minette shared her passionate nature: she feared this emotionalism and tried to restrain it. So Minette's longing for outward signs of her mother's affection was constantly repressed. On one occasion, the child's vivid imagination, which readily encouraged her to think that possible dangers were realities, led her to fear that her mother's indisposition was going to prove fatal. In response, Mme Necker told her: 'I am coughing a little, my dear, but I should indeed prefer it if you did not exaggerate, even in matters of feeling'. Particularly adept at a kind of moral blackmail, Mme Necker succeeded in instilling into her daughter an ineradicable sense of guilt. It is not surprising that her Minette would ultimately revolt against this maternal form of repression, and that she would come to extol naturalness, spontaneity and freedom above all.

Meanwhile, Minette was just two years old when her mother introduced her to the Bible and works of devotion. According to Mme Necker, the child was to be brought up — in theory — in the manner of Rousseau's Emile, not his Sophie (a girl confined to those subjects thought proper for her sex, subjects that would make her fit to be Emile's helpmeet). Mme Necker overlooked the fact that Emile was to stay in the country air and was not to read books before he was twelve. So, along with the masterpieces of seventeenth-century French literature and more recent works of poetry and ideas, she taught Minette Latin and English. The child was said to speak English fluently by the time she was twelve years old. She would be well acquainted with English literature, with the poetry of Milton and Gray, and with the novels of Fielding and Richardson (the elopement of Richardson's deceived Clarissa with the rake Lovelace being 'one of the events' of Minette's early years). Mme Necker also instructed her in mathematics and theology, history and geography. The girl soon knew how to think for herself and express herself with ease. She had to answer questions like 'What is the best government?'.

19

In reply, she asserted that it was certainly not government by one man alone, but a system which allowed people to live in independence.

In 1776, at the age of ten, she accompanied her parents on a visit to England that lasted six weeks. There, she went with them to call on Horace Walpole and Edward Gibbon (with whom her mother was reconciled). She was taken into the Houses of Parliament. At the theatre, on several occasions she saw Garrick in Shakespeare. The great actor 'was kind enough to be pleased with the ecstasy his performance aroused in me', she recalled later. The Neckers were also acquainted with Elizabeth Montagu, the well-known Shakespearian critic whose devotion to the dramatist they shared.

Back in Paris, visitors to Mme Necker's salon used to find young Minette seated on a stool placed next to her mother's armchair. From time to time her mother would admonish her to sit up straight. Among the eminent gentlemen who addressed the girl solicitously were the poet Thomas and the novelist and dramatist Marmontel. A man in a little round wig took her hands in his, and conversed with her as if she were twenty-five. This was abbé Raynal, the famous opponent of superstition and tyranny. During dinner, the girl said nothing, 'but you should have seen how Mlle Necker listened! Her eyes followed the movements of the speakers and seemed to be ahead of their ideas'. She was being observed by Catherine Huber, a girl who had been carefully selected to be her companion, and whom she welcomed effusively as a friend. According to Catherine Huber, she grasped everything, even political subjects which at that time were already occupying a good deal of the conversation.

After dinner, many more guests arrived and all, on approaching Mme Necker, addressed a compliment or a witticism to her daughter, who replied with easy grace. Some, including the most noted wits, took pleasure in provoking the girl to respond or in stimulating her lively imagination. Apparently, Mme Necker did not object: she saw all this 'as a kind of gymnastics of the intellectual faculties'. Others did not agree. That moralizing novelist, Mme de Genlis (future spy for Napoleon), who never cared for the Neckers, coldly remarked that Mlle Necker had been badly brought up by her mother. This was because, while the mother's attention was elsewhere, wits held conversations with the girl on the passions, especially love, and other matters Mme de Genlis thought well beyond her years.

In appearance, so it was generally agreed, Mlle Necker was not especially attractive. Her complexion was too swarthy for the taste of her time. But her huge eyes, her dominant feature, illuminated her face. The artist (and dramatist) Carmontelle sketched her at thirteen, revealing her warmly vivacious expression. There she sits stiffly, her hands demurely folded in her lap, tightly laced in whalebone, in a beribboned bodice, her hair teased into heavy curls over her ears and piled high on her head as if to resemble a powdered wig. She looks rather like an animated doll. Somewhat tactlessly, her father was to inform her that her appearance left something to be desired and that she could only hope for success of a serious and solid kind. 'My daughter is amiable without being beautiful', Mme Necker would inform Edward Gibbon. The girl was to confide to her diary: ' . . . these glances of mine into the mirror are not due to vanity but are an attempt to reassure myself'. No wonder she would need constant proof of her power to hold a man's affections.

Vain and self-regarding she certainly was. How could it be otherwise, when she served as the centre of attention and an object of flattery for the celebrities of the day? They prompted her desire to equal or surpass them in *gloire* or fame. At the same time, she was extremely vulnerable. When her impulses and emotions, held in precarious check by her mother, found an outlet, their intensity was such that they passed, as it were, beyond their object. And this pattern was to recur throughout her life. There was one moment, for instance, when Mme Huber, intending to visit the Bois de Boulogne with her daughter Catherine, offered to take Mlle Necker with them. The offer took Mme Necker by surprise. As she hesitated, Minette watched, full of fear and hope. Permission was granted, to the girl's extreme joy. Meanwhile, Mme Necker gave detailed instructions about the various precautions to be taken with the carriage, for this was the first time the girl had ever gone anywhere without her mother. The very idea of this outing left Minette in a fever of impatient anticipation. When Mme Huber arrived for the drive to the Bois, the girl kissed her hands and threw herself on her neck. She did not see the woods, the carriages, the elegant promenaders, 'she saw only her own happiness and was absorbed solely in that', observed her friend, Catherine Huber.

From an early age, Minette had acquired a dread of loneliness. As an intelligent only child with a death-haunted mother, she would rapidly perceive that her parents, the sole beings who made her universe, who loved her totally and whom she loved, were fragile creatures subject to mortality. The unutterable fear of being left alone became an obsession. Once, when her mother was briefly absent, the girl wrote her a forlorn letter: 'My dear Mamma, . . . in this great house which only a short while ago enclosed all I held dear, and where my entire world and my future were confined, I now see nothing but a waste land. For the first time I realized that this expanse was too large for me, and I ran into my little room, so that my eyes could at least take in the surrounding void. Your brief absence has made me tremble for my fate . . .'. Mme Necker's only reaction to this cry for help was to criticize the style of her daughter's letter and the lack of taste in its expression of feeling. Yet the fear of emptiness and nothingness would remain with Necker's daughter throughout her life. Long after both her parents were dead and when she was indeed alone, she tormented herself with the thought of isolation and absence, trying to fill the void with social intercourse, with ceaseless action and activity, and making demands on others in the vain hope that they might assuage her ennui and her dread, support her and help her to face the hollowness and the pain of existence. Often she was to reflect on suicide, flirt with it, employ it as a weapon, deeply impressed as she was by Goethe's *Werther*, which she read in translation, and which inaugurated a veritable fashion for self-destruction.

Concentrated studies, her indoor life, her over-excitable nature finally led the girl into a decline. The worried parents called in the famous Dr Tronchin, who prescribed fresh air, and an end to lessons and the wearing of whalebone. Necker had bought a fine residence at Saint-Ouen, outside Paris, and thither Minette was dispatched with a governess and maid. For the first time, she was free of her mother's constant supervision, and made a rapid recovery. Each Friday, Catherine Huber came to visit her and relieve the tedium of country life, for Minette cared little for the pleasures of the countryside. During the weekend, the girls played at huntresses (trying to imitate a ballet they had seen at the Opéra), and inscribed verses on tree trunks in pastoral style.

Minette wrote a play which the two girls and the servants performed to great acclaim in front of her parents and all their friends who came from Paris to see it.

Now that his daughter was of an age to be interesting, Necker himself began to take more notice of her existence. He needed relaxation from the complex and insoluble financial affairs of the nation, and he would say to his wife, 'Let's go and see Minette'. By the time he was obliged to resign his post in May 1781, and the great nobles and clergy, the financiers and men of letters drove out in their carriages to express their sympathy, the transfer of her affections to her father was complete. Mme Necker could see only too clearly what was happening. Once, having left the dining-room, she returned to find her husband and her daughter chasing each other laughing round the table, with napkins tied as turbans round their heads. Under Mme Necker's disapproving eye, they went back to their places in silence. The girl's natural high spirits, which did battle with her melancholy temperament, prompted a quick response in her father, who doubtless found his daughter's company a relief after his wife's morbidity and self-imposed constraint.

Mme Necker kept a record of her own shortcomings, in which she noted her irritation with her husband and her servants. There, she complained about his lack of attentiveness. True, he was a generous and sensitive husband who did not encroach on her freedom and who loved her, but not quite with the love she wished for herself, 'although he is convinced of it and I let others believe it'. So much for the picture of the ideal marriage she sedulously cultivated in public. To Necker, she wrote: 'I have plainly seen from what you say that you disapproved of my feelings and my conduct towards your daughter . . .'. By degrees, mother and daughter might be regarded as virtual rivals for Necker's affections, a situation obliquely represented in the play the young woman was later to write in poor verse entitled *Sophie, or the Secret Feelings*. There, Miss Sophie Mortimer, the melancholy orphaned heroine, rejects an offer of marriage from the estimable milord Henri Bedford because she is all unknowingly in love with her married guardian, the comte de Sainville. The latter's outwardly reserved but passionate wife discovers Sophie's secret inclination for her husband, and then, finding out that he dotes on his ward, falls in a faint. All ends in a contest of

23

magnanimity and self-sacrifice.

Minette idolized her father who petted and indulged her, and who now needed her to relieve the tensions of office or the disappointments of his fall from power. The contrast between his affectionate teasing and his reliability as an ally on the one hand, and on the other her mother's rejection of the girl's desire for a show of affection, was too great. She felt a tender respect for her mother which concealed a growing spirit of rebellion, later made manifest in the ambivalent portrayal of 'bad' or narrow-minded mother-figures in her fiction. Her mother had wanted to educate her so that she would be not only the prodigy but the exemplar of the age. When congratulated on the success of her efforts, Mme Necker would reply rather sourly, 'It is nothing, absolutely nothing, in comparison with what I wanted to make of her'.

As for the girl herself, she longed to be or to do something outstanding that would gratify her father. The cautious, indecisive, rather self-satisfied Necker appeared to her as the embodiment of the truly great man, sincere, high-minded, just; one who believed that there was no separation to be made between morality and politics; a man against whom all others were to be judged. It is scarcely surprising that none would be able to stand for long in the light of this paragon.

The girl's upbringing and education led her to value naturalness not only in contrast to her mother's sense of discipline and control, but also in response to her father's dislike of affectation. To insist on spontaneity as a virtue was to thwart her mother while at the same time indulging her own impetuous nature, without always having regard to the possible consequences of her impulsive actions. She had acquired through her mother's teaching an impressive capacity for analysis, for reasoning, for comparing, which would make her deeply aware of certain realities that underlay the trends of the age, while at the same time she would have a poor grasp of the everyday conduct of existence as carried on gingerly by most human beings.

Alongside her gift of analysis there was, too, her power of imagination, and her strong idealizing faculty which was encouraged by the literature and the art of her era. Just as she idealized her father, so she would idealize with passionate intensity her friends and everybody she loved. Only her father largely — though not entirely — escaped the scalpel of her analysis. The

24

strange thing is that in the very process of idealizing others she would soon be fully aware of their weaknesses and shortcomings, an awareness that she would try to suppress for as long as she could in the interests of her imaginative ideal.

3 Marriage of an Heiress

From an early age, Mlle Necker was on the marriage market. The negotiations for her hand, in which several courts in Europe were interested, and which lasted over a period of five years, give some idea of the status of Jacques Necker or perhaps, more realistically, of the attraction of his fortune. The marriage was no easy matter to settle, however. First, there was the question of religion: the Neckers were determined that their daughter's future husband must be a Protestant. Second, they had set their sights high, and required a person of rank and position. To make the affair more complicated, the girl did not wish to have to live far from her parents, nor did she want to leave France and especially her beloved Paris.

In 1778, when Minette was twelve, an application was received from Eric Magnus Staël von Holstein, who was then twenty-nine, and attached to the Swedish Embassy in Paris. The Neckers were not keen: true, he was a Protestant, but he had prospects rather than position. The seventh son of a captain in the Swedish army, of ancient family but little means, Eric Magnus had volunteered for the soldier's life at sixteen. He had managed to attract the attention of his king, Gustavus III, who was inclined to favour handsome young men. In Paris, he was taken under the wing of the Swedish Ambassador who, impressed with the young officer's discretion and judgement, began to consider him seriously as his future successor. The dashing diplomat also rapidly conquered the hearts of Parisian ladies of rank and influence, a number of whom — including Mme de Boufflers, a close friend of Gustavus III — devoted themselves to his advancement. Not least among his patronesses was Marie-Antoinette herself, in love with the Swedish Count Axel Fersen. High life in Paris was expensive: young Staël had soon run into considerable debt, so that he urgently needed to make a rich marriage. He had no title, but adopted or was granted in France the courtesy title of Baron de Staël.

Meanwhile, over the years, other suitors presented themselves. Among them was a prince who candidly declared that his financial affairs were 'in an extremely disorderly state'. Necker managed to evade this unambiguous offer for the dowry in a diplomatic manner. At one stage, in 1783, there was much talk of William Pitt the Younger as prospective husband for Mlle Necker. A youthful Chancellor of the Exchequer, Pitt was already, in 1783, at the age of twenty-five, Prime Minister. The girl's parents seem to have taken the prospect of this alliance more seriously than Pitt himself. Mme Necker in particular favoured the English politician, but her daughter would have none of him, and each had sharp words for the other. What the girl dreaded was the prospect of having to leave Paris and spend the rest of her life in England.

It looked as if Staël remained the only serious contender, since he stayed steadily in the field throughout. The deadlock reached in the Staël negotiations has been neatly summed up in the formula: 'no marriage, no embassy; no embassy, no marriage'. Facing ruin from his mounting debts, Staël wrote plaintively to his sovereign who, however, declined to make him ambassador in Paris before the marriage took place. Instead, Gustavus III asked him to obtain the island of Tobago in the Lesser Antilles for Sweden if he wanted to be ambassador. With great effort, Staël managed to acquire the island of St Bartholomew (which remained Swedish to 1878). The king did not consider this small island sufficient to entitle his protégé to the Paris embassy for more than six years. The whole affair was nearly off.

Necker plainly stated his conditions: Staël was to be Swedish ambassador in Paris for life: he was to be made a count and decorated with a high order; he was to receive a pension should he lose the embassy; his future wife was not to be taken to Sweden unless she herself wished it; and the queen of France was to state that she desired the marriage to take place. The king of Sweden was annoyed. He told Mme de Boufflers, who was conducting the delicate negotiations, that he found the former finance minister's pretentions 'exorbitant, to say the least'. Were they treating for the marriage of some great French princess? asked King Gustavus sarcastically. It was scarcely very flattering to himself and his compatriots that Mlle Necker never wanted to settle in his country. Of course, had she been inclined to do so, his royal desire that her fortune should accrue to Sweden might serve as a pretext to colour his gracious condescension to Necker. He could not help adding that 'there are forms of respect to be observed towards a queen of France, towards myself, and M. Necker, however lofty and wealthy he may be, has not the right to dispense with them'. It seemed as if the matter was going to rest there. None the less, Marie-Antoinette remained anxious to settle the girl's marriage with Staël as soon as possible since her lover, Count Fersen, had asked for Mlle Necker's hand.

In the autumn of 1784, the Neckers travelled to the south of France with a large retinue of servants. They wintered in Avignon and Montpellier. Mme Necker's health was causing alarm, and it was thought that a warmer climate might help to restore her. Mlle Necker attended provincial balls, where she enjoyed being courted and having verses penned in her honour. She saw through 'all these admirers' who, unless they were already married or had taken vows, were only too frequently 'dreaming of my dowry'.

By the autumn of 1785, a compromise had been reached between Gustavus III and Jacques Necker, and the marriage was arranged. Mlle Necker settled for Staël, now officially granted the title of baron that he had been using, who was to receive a huge dowry. If some people thought the union was good enough for the upstart Neckers, this was certainly not the opinion of Catherine II of Russia (a great admirer of the financier), who remarked that it was a 'very wretched marriage'.

Staël might be elegant and experienced in amours, but he was stiff and studied with his betrothed, while she had few illusions about him and his motives. It was clear to her that he lacked imaginative scope: 'He is a perfect gentleman, incapable of saying or doing anything stupid, but unproductive and slack', she confided to her diary in 1785. How could she forget what happened at the ball when her father invited M. de Staël to dance with her? She was at once struck by the frigidity of her future husband's manner. Suddenly, Necker exclaimed: 'Wait, sir, I am going to show you how to dance with a young lady with whom one is in love'. The comparison was too much for her: she fled to a corner of the room in tears, and her father followed her and embraced her. 'What a fortunate creature I should have been if a fourth person as pictured in my heart had come to join us; if it had been a great man who admired my father, a sensitive soul who loved me . . . !', she wrote in her diary. 'What delight to have as husband one whose step, whose voice would make my heart beat faster!' But it was no use dreaming of a second Necker who would love her for, as she observed in her portrait of her father, written in August 1785, 'two men like you cannot be found within the possibilities of the same destiny . . .'. She could not help recording in her diary her deep regret that she was unable to marry 'a great man; it is the sole glory of a woman on this earth . . .'.

On 6 January 1786, the marriage contract was signed at Versailles by Louis XVI, Marie-Antoinette, and the princes of the blood. Eight days later, the wedding was solemnized in the chapel of the Swedish embassy. The bride was nineteen (rather older than most convent-bred brides of that period), the groom thirty-seven. It has been aptly said that he married Necker's millions and she married Paris.

According to custom, the newly-weds passed the first days of marriage under the parental roof. Before leaving, Mme de Staël wrote a sorrowful letter to her sick mother: 'My dear Mamma, . . . I submit to my fate . . . happiness if possible will come later, at intervals, or never . . .'. This was scarcely the letter of a contented bride. It was not long before she would be completely disillusioned with the institution of marriage. 'Don't you find it odd that one should pay so dearly for the honour a man has done you in spending a few wretched nights with you? Oh! How I thoroughly loathe marriage!', she was to say dryly, some years afterwards.

The marriage ceremony was followed by her formal presentation at court on 31 January 1786. Only too often inclined to fail in some particular where matters of strict etiquette were concerned, Mme de Staël arrived late at Versailles, tripped on descending hastily from her carriage, and tore her dress. Then, on making her third curtsy to Marie-Antoinette and bending low to kiss the hem of the queen's robe, the trimmings of her own train came off. The king smiled, graciously trying to cover any embarrassment on the young woman's part: 'If you are not at ease with us, you will not be so anywhere else', he said, while the queen took her into a boudoir where a maid repaired the damage. 'She had little success', commented one aristocratic lady haughtily. 'Everyone found her ugly, awkward, above all, affected', with the airs of a Genevan upstart.

As for Mme de Boufflers, who had brought the tedious marriage negotiations to a successful conclusion, she could be found writing with undisguised malice to Gustavus III that, unlike the socially accomplished ambassador, Mme de Staël

> has no acquaintance with the customs and manners of society . . . . She is domineering and excessively opinionated; she has a self-assurance such as I have never seen in anyone else at any age and of any rank; she argues about everything without rhyme or reason and, though she has wit . . . you could count twenty things out of place for one good point in what she says.

Though lauded to the skies by her father's supporters, added Mme de Boufflers, those who were more impartial blamed her for 'talking too much, being too self-assured, and showing more wit than common sense and tact'. It was rather late in the day for informing the Swedish monarch that he had been advised to favour a marriage where his ambassadress was indiscreet and his ambassador unwilling or unable to control his own wife.

Meanwhile, Germaine had set herself the task of making the most of the role of ambassadress. She even began to learn Swedish. To Gustavus III, she sent entertaining reports in French. While regularly attending her mother's salon, she now held her own gatherings at the embassy in the rue du Bac. To it there would be drawn not only diplomats like Thomas Jefferson (later third president of the United States), but also the cream of the French liberal-minded aristocracy, including the marquis de La Fayette, hero of the American War of Independence; the marquis de Condorcet; Talleyrand (then bishop of Autun); the comte de Guibert; and her life-long friend, Mathieu de Montmorency. They were attracted by her vivacity and her fascinating conversation, an outpouring of ideas on all subjects, expressed with inimitable charm and ease.

Mme de Staël's success as the hostess of her own salon is reflected in the portrait of her as Zulmé, penned by her admirer, the comte de Guibert, and supposedly translated from the Greek:

> Zulmé is only twenty, and she is the most famous priestess of Apollo. . . . Her great dark eyes sparkled with genius; her ebony-coloured hair fell over her shoulders in waving curls; her

features were strong rather than delicate; one felt in them the presence of something higher than the destiny of her sex. . . .

After singing Apollo's praises, Zulmé put down her lyre and discoursed upon the great truths of nature, the immortality of the soul, the love of liberty. She seemed to be many people in one. 'I find in her charms superior to beauty. What animation and variety of expression! . . .' At the general applause, Zulmé inclined her head modestly. This portrait in words, where Zulmé is compared to advantage with the Pythia of Delphi and the Sibyl of Cumae, resembles that of some muse or demi-goddess depicted by a neo-classical painter of the age. Its details were to make a deep impression on Germaine's imagination and on the way she conceived her ideal self.

The attentions paid to his wife by the gallant ex-soldier, the comte de Guibert, began to disturb M. de Staël, who believed — doubtless wrongly — that this authority on military affairs and man of letters was her lover. M. de Guibert, who had known her since childhood, was rather vain and twenty years her senior. She seems to have confided in him, telling him about her disappointments in marriage. He certainly shared her concern for political reform. Germaine was not at all pleased when M. de Staël began to adopt what she called 'husbandly airs'.

Besides, she was pregnant. Her first child, named Gustavine, god-daughter of the king and queen of Sweden, was born on 22 July 1787. Little is known about Mme de Staël's attitude to her first-born, whom she decided not to nurse, and whom she placed in the care of servants. No doubt it was similar to that of the ladies of her circle. The child, who was to die nearly two years later, did not interfere with Germaine's dreams and ambitions.

Whatever her social activity and triumphs, the self-absorbed Germaine was always subject to attacks of deep melancholy and morbid dread: ' . . . often in solitude, the emptiness of my heart fills my eyes with tears'. Melancholy might be concealed under social gaiety, but she would always regard it as a powerful source of imaginative inspiration. It was in the years of her betrothal and marriage that she wrote a number of prose tales, including *Histoire de Pauline* and *Mirza*, about ill-fated heroines; the weak verse plays, *Sophie* and *Jane Gray*; and her *Letters on the Writings and Character of Jean-Jacques Rousseau*, which, published in a limited edition in 1788, announced the arrival of a writer who could already command serious attention.

The 'emptiness' of her heart was to be filled by a brief affair with Talleyrand, which doubtless meant rather more to her than to him. A notorious womanizer, the crippled and embittered Talleyrand, who equalled her as a brilliant talker, was to rise to eminence through the Directory, the Consulate, the First Empire, the Restoration and beyond, a byword for corruption and machiavellism, and the very opposite of all that Mme de Staël would stand for. It was Talleyrand, it seems, who introduced her to a great friend of his, comte Louis de Narbonne-Lara, with whom she was to embark upon a grand drama of love and ambition.

4 Revolution: the Quest for Happiness

Though unhappy in her marriage, young Germaine still ardently believed in the possibility of happiness, for which she yearned. Had not the American founding fathers proclaimed every person's right to happiness? This revolutionary notion swiftly spread across the Atlantic to shake the old regime rooted in obedience and obligation. The ruthless Saint-Just, only slightly younger than Germaine herself, was to call happiness a new idea in Europe. For her, happiness appeared to lie in the union of love with power.

She realized that, in her world, there could be no way for her to acquire power and influence except through the career of a man, preferably 'a great man'. It soon became obvious to her that her husband's aspirations were limited. As the daughter of Necker, she was courted by those who wanted to reach her father, but there was no question of her influencing him in his decisions. In effect, she was to move well beyond Necker in her opinions as a reformer and in her political goals.

The person who would dominate her life for five years, changing it utterly, was a man of great promise and unfulfilled ambition, a supreme product of the old regime. Louis de Narbonne, whom she tried to propel to the forefront of the political arena, charmed all who met him as an elegant wit, a handsome and dashing officer. Many believed him to be the illegitimate son of Louis XV. Well known for his roving eye and his numerous feminine conquests, Louis de Narbonne had married an heiress whose wealth ultimately proved insufficient to meet his pressing debts. It might well appear to the cynical of the day that some goodly part of Germaine's attraction for the irresistible Narbonne, aside from her vivacious intelligence and inimitable conversation, was the access she provided to Necker and Necker's fortune.

It was upon this dazzling aristocrat, eleven years her senior, that Germaine fastened her single-minded bid for happiness. No matter that her mother had warned her against aristocratic libertines in general and against Narbonne in particular, at the very moment when Germaine was making her début in society. As a girl, she had gleaned from literature the idea that passionate love was the supreme purpose of a woman's life, and that it meant total absorption in the beloved, his well-being, his interests. It also implied, she felt, the sacrifice of one's own considerations and concerns, and the unswerving devotion of the slave. In return for this submission of the feminine partner, the object of her affections was expected to meet like with like, and to provide unfailing protection and support. In this way, feminine submission also spelt domination, as she well knew.

Germaine's affair with Narbonne began in the autumn of 1788, not long after Necker was recalled to the Ministry of Finance. It developed in the months leading up to the French Revolution, and in the first years of the upheaval, providing a private counterpoint to public events.

On 5 May 1789, Germaine was present at the opening of the States General. No wonder she felt elated, for this body had not met in public session since 1614. The day before, she watched excitedly from a window as the representatives of the three estates walked in procession to hear mass. She was especially impressed by the members of the third estate — consisting of lawyers, financiers, men of letters (for the lower orders had no voice in affairs) — dressed in sober black. Walking along with them were those nobles who also served as representatives of the third estate, including the imposing comte de Mirabeau.

Once the delegates to the States General transformed it into the National Assembly, and the oath was taken in the tennis-court, the Revolution had begun its headlong course. Although the decision to call the States General had been adopted when Necker was out of office, the advocates of privilege blamed him for it and its consequences. The king was persuaded to dismiss Necker but, well aware of his minister's popularity, commanded him to go into exile in secret. Necker and his wife left at once in the clothes they were wearing for Brussels, where Mme de Staël joined them and accompanied them to Basle. No sooner had her father's disgrace become known than people took to the streets, clamouring for his return.

It was in Basle that Necker learned of his recall. Such were the hopes placed in him that, on the road back to Paris, women knelt in the fields as the Neckers' carriage passed; in the towns, men untied the horses and drew the vehicle along themselves. By the time the Neckers entered Paris, people stood at the windows, on the roofs, in the streets, shouting 'Vive Monsieur Necker!' Germaine was intoxicated by the public acclamations at the Hôtel de Ville. This was true fame, this was *gloire*. She never forgot that day. As for Necker himself, he was more far-seeing than his daughter. He told his brother: 'It seems to me that I am returning to be swallowed in the abyss'. He was right: all his efforts were to be thwarted by the king's weakness and the machinations of the court party.

Necker did not want revolution: his aim was a constitutional monarchy on a firm financial basis, and the reform of notorious abuses. But he could provide only temporary palliatives. It was his daughter who was fascinated and thrilled by the prospect of some great transformation for the better, although she too did not envisage the destruction of the monarchy. Germaine de Staël was the first woman writer to sense the sheer poetry of political action, that extraordinary sensation which seized writers and intellectuals during the French Revolution, and which has never ceased to recur at intervals since then. She was to say: 'To apply oneself to politics is religion, moral science and poetry all together'. Here was her great opportunity to participate, if only at second hand, in the deliberations of the Constituent Assembly, through the delegates who attended her salon. Often, seated among the numerous spectators in the gallery of the Assembly, she could be observed listening avidly to the debates, thrilling to what she called 'the electricity of ideas'. If she ever yearned to be among the speakers, she did not say so, nor did she mention the possibility of active female participation as the obscure Théroigne de Méricourt was to do.

At that period, and up to the end of 1791, political affairs were largely in the hands of an aristocratic élite, men who combined the elegant manners of the old regime with a deep love of freedom. Noblemen who were more proud of their enlightened outlook than of their caste or privileges (which they hastened to resign), mingled with gifted representatives of the third estate in

Germaine's salon. These were the men with whom she discussed in her piquant way the political ideas and affairs of the moment. She invited to her dinner parties both royalists and libertarians in the hope, vain as it was to prove, that they might reach some amicable compromise. Afterwards, she was convinced that 'never was seen so much life and wit . . .'. This was the moment when she was seized by the illusion of untrammelled happiness — happiness for all the citizens, and happiness for the individual, such as she felt she knew with Narbonne.

Among the matters being discussed with such fervour and excitement in Mme de Staël's circle were many that are now all too often taken for granted by people who to-day enjoy these hard-won advances of the human spirit — benefits which are still ignored or repudiated even now in various parts of the globe. The longed-for reforms embraced individual freedom and civil rights for all; equality before the law, trial by jury, legal guarantees (such as the right to public trial, to have defence counsel and to confront witnesses); division of the executive and legislative powers; elections, freedom of the press, freedom of worship, the abolition of torture such as breaking on the wheel.

Many of the reforms advocated by Mme de Staël and her friends were adopted by the Constituent Assembly. There was to be no taxation without representation; feudal rights, castes and privileges were abolished and, along with them, all those pernicious taxes of the old regime which burdened the peasantry, like the *corvée* or forced labour. Advancement in professions like the army was no longer to be the prerogative of the aristocracy but open to any person of ability. 'At last', she was to remark later, 'a nation long bound to the soil arose, as it were, from beneath the earth . . .', liberated from 'the triple chain of an intolerant church, a feudal nobility and a limitless royal authority'.

While discussions were taking place that so enthralled Mme de Staël, famine and hardship gnawed at the poorer classes, far beyond Necker's power to alleviate. Irrational fears took hold. Rumours were rife. Believing that the king was in league with foreign powers and that he was about to leave the country, an angry mob marched on the palace of Versailles on 5 October 1789. As soon as Mme de Staël heard what was happening, early that morning, she left Paris at once by a side road to join her parents at Versailles. The king was out hunting as usual, and had to be called back to the palace. During the night, some of the armed rebels penetrated almost as far as the queen's bedchamber, killing a number of her bodyguards. The horrified Mme de Staël saw the bloodstains. The people were demanding the king's return to the capital, and he, his wife and family were conveyed by the armed populace to the barely habitable Tuileries palace, which had not been occupied for years.

Looking back on these events, Mme de Staël perceived that the aim of the Revolution was changing from liberty to equality. It seemed to her, born into the middle class but the favoured product of an aristocratic society, that the illiterate and the deprived were not yet ready to participate in affairs — a role she reserved for the enlightened. For her, the word 'liberty' presented no ambiguities; whereas she was convinced that abstract equality (as distinct from equality before the law and equality of opportunity) remained impossible to define or to put into practice.

From that day, the monarchy was fixed on its downward path. Necker, however, remained faithful to the king (who did not heed his advice), and this loyalty cost him his popularity, outstripped as he now was in popular favour by Mirabeau and La Fayette. On 3 September 1790, Necker resigned, depositing in the royal treasury the sum of two million francs, part of his private fortune, and receiving the king's bond for its ultimate return. He left with his wife for Coppet, the handsome mansion not far from Geneva which he had purchased some years earlier, and where he would spend the rest of his life in melancholy reflection.

Germaine had just given birth to a son, Auguste, acknowledged by M. de Staël as his own, but in actuality her first child by Narbonne. Already, relations with her parents were severely strained. Mme Necker, with her strict standards of dutiful conduct, was outraged by her erring daughter's association with Narbonne, promising her that it would not come to good. She made no secret of her feelings to Necker, who could not help expressing his disapproval in his own way. But Germaine was entirely absorbed in her passion for Narbonne and, for her lover's benefit, she would even venture to criticize her father. Necker now took second place.

Having spent the autumn of 1790 miserably with her parents in

Switzerland, Germaine returned to Paris in January 1791, no longer under the protective shadow of her once powerful father. It was in her salon that the new Constitution of 1791 was formulated — the very system which she would later criticize for weakening the monarchy. At this time, she professed a great admiration for that self-appointed lawgiver, abbé Sieyès (author of the pamphlet 'What is the Third Estate?'), who could often be found in her salon, a general meeting-place for moderate reformers. In April 1791, Germaine published an unsigned political article in her friend Suard's paper, *Les Indépendants*, entitled 'By what tokens can the opinion of the majority of the nation be recognized?'. She doubtless published others which have not all come to light. It is believed that she contributed to Talleyrand's speech on the death of Mirabeau, and also to his report on public education, especially the section concerning the education of women and the passage on human perfectibility.

Mme de Staël had set her mind on achieving a high government post for Narbonne. She had left Coppet for Paris not long after the abortive flight of Louis XVI and his family, their arrest at Varennes, and their ignominious return to the capital. In this bungled affair Gustavus III and his agent, Count Fersen, were involved, and the Swedish ambassador was therefore left in an embarrassing position. M. de Staël found consolation, however, with the great classical actress, Mlle Clairon, then over sixty, who had once taught Germaine declamation. To Mlle Clairon he allotted a large pension, well beyond his means, a course which would eventually lead to his financial ruin. The intricate political and private affairs of M. and Mme de Staël kept malicious tongues in Paris wagging.

When Germaine contrived to have Narbonne appointed Minister of War on 6 December 1791, the queen commented savagely to her lover Fersen: 'What glory for Mme de Staël, and what pleasure for her to have the entire army . . . to herself'. While Germaine was dreaming that her lover might save the country, her enemies were denouncing her to the king as the 'dangerous woman' who kept Narbonne under her thumb. As always, pamphleteers and satirists liked to stress sexual misconduct. A caricaturist depicted Mme de Staël with the courtesan Théroigne de Méricourt as 'the principal sluts who have played a prone role in the Revolution'. Her name was often linked with Théroigne's, both being regarded as courtesans who were aiming at political influence.

As Minister of War, Narbonne at once strove to reorganize the army, then in disarray, in order to defend the frontiers. But three months later he was forced from office, followed shortly by the entire ministry under attack from the Girondins. If Talleyrand is to be believed, Germaine wrote Narbonne's speeches, and even his reports on the state of the army. In all likelihood, she exerted no little influence on them.

Mme de Staël, along with Narbonne, suggested a new plan for the royal family to escape to England. It was rejected by Marie-Antoinette. Soon, it was too late. Throughout the night of 9 August 1792, Germaine heard the lugubrious tolling of the tocsin, and early in the morning of 10 August the sound of cannon fire. Out she drove, anxious to learn what was happening at the Tuileries palace. Her coachman was stopped on the bridge by men who silently made the ritual sign that people were having their throats cut on the Right Bank. All her friends, the constitutional monarchists, she discovered, had gone into hiding. So she set out on foot to see what she could do to help them.

It was on 10 August that the Republic was proclaimed. In the days that followed, when Austrian and Prussian troops crossed the frontier, people were being arrested and charged with treachery because of their class, their dress or their opinions. The prisons were full. Somehow, Germaine found extraordinary reserves of courage. The fact that she was pregnant did not in any way curtail her activity on behalf of her friends. She hid Narbonne and others in the Swedish embassy. A servant told her that a poster denouncing Narbonne had been affixed at the corner of the street. When the revolutionary guards came to search the embassy, she managed to persuade them that the house enjoyed diplomatic immunity. A friend of hers from Hanover risked his life to take Narbonne to safety in England.

Meanwhile, she learned that her friends, Lally-Tollendal and Jaucourt, were in prison under threat of execution. She decided to apply to Manuel, one of the leading members of the Governing Committee of the Commune — soon to be proclaimed the National Convention — a man whose literary pretentions (she thought) might conceivably predispose him in her favour. At seven in the morning, before Manuel was out of bed, she was waiting for him in his study. Her appeal moved him to intercede for Jaucourt, whose release he obtained (Lally-Tollendal having been freed through another's good offices). After this drama, Germaine thought she had better leave in haste for Switzerland: she had promised to collect abbé de Montesquiou outside the city gate and take him with her disguised as one of her servants.

Then she miscalculated. She thought that if she travelled in her six-horse carriage emblazoned with the Swedish coat of arms, and with her servants in grand livery, such ostentation would impress upon the lower orders the idea that the ambassadress had every right to depart. Scarcely had she set off when some 'old women from hell' hurled themselves upon the horses, crying out that she was taking the country's gold to the enemy. At once, a fierce-looking crowd gathered round, forcing her postilions to stop, and compelling her to go to the local revolutionary tribunal (the faubourg Saint-Germain sector). She just managed to whisper to abbé de Montesquiou's servant to run and warn his master. Someone had denounced her for trying to leave Paris with proscribed members of the aristocracy, and Narbonne in particular. 'You have helped Narbonne to escape!' went the cry.

The local tribunal ordered that she must be conveyed to the Hôtel de Ville, where the Governing Committee was in session. It took three hours to get there from the faubourg Saint-Germain. With one exception, her guards were unmoved by her condition. At the Hôtel de Ville, she climbed the stairs through a hostile mob armed with pikes, and entered the courtroom crowded with jostling humanity. Presiding over the court sat the ruthless apostle of virtue, Robespierre (with whom she had chatted only two years before at her father's). Manuel vouched for her, leading her and her chamber-maid into his office, where she waited for him for six hours, with nothing to eat or drink.

At last, Manuel came and took her home through darkened streets. She was granted a new passport for herself and her chamber-maid. Next day, Tallien, a member of the Governing Committee like Manuel, arrived to take her to the Swiss frontier. In her house, Tallien caught sight of several aristocrats whose lives were in danger. She begged him to say nothing about them, and he kept his promise.

Once at Coppet, Germaine busied herself trying to save her friends: some she would manage to keep hidden nearby under

Swedish names. Recalcitrant Swiss officials were persuaded by her to turn a blind eye if the unfortunate's passport were not correct in every particular. Despite all her efforts, she was not always successful; nor were all those she rescued, then and later, as grateful as they should have been.

To join Narbonne in England: that was her one desire. But the journey was too dangerous for a woman advanced in pregnancy. On 20 November 1792, she gave birth to Albert, her second son by Narbonne. Eager to be up and about, she wrote to her lover: 'I overturn all kinds of etiquette in these matters'. Means had to be found to help clear Narbonne's huge debts, and it was with Mme de Staël's financial help that Narbonne and his close friend and aide-de-camp, General d'Arblay, along with Lally-Tollendal, Jaucourt and the faithful Mathieu de Montmorency, were enabled to live at Juniper Hall, near Dorking in Surrey.

Leaving her two small children, Auguste and Albert, at Coppet (much to her parents' vocal disapproval and contempt for her conduct), Germaine arrived at Juniper Hall in January 1793. The little French community of constitutional monarchists, delightful birds of exotic plumage, had already caused a flutter in this quiet rural backwater. Among the fascinated inhabitants, touched by the misfortunes of their visitors, was Mrs Susanna Phillips, sister of the novelist Fanny Burney. Germaine's arrival caused an explosion. 'She is one of the first women I have ever met with for abilities and extraordinary intellects', wrote the author of *Evelina* to her father, Dr Burney, the eminent musicologist. 'We are very good friends', said Miss Burney, who found Mme de Staël's open-hearted warmth 'impossible to resist'. Everyone was astonished when Germaine read her reflections on happiness, that subject of the hour, part of the first draft of her great study, *On the Influence of the Passions upon the Happiness of Individuals and of Nations*, undertaken to distract her mind from the general horrors of September 1792. Delighted with Miss Burney, Germaine pressed her to stay longer.

Dreadful rumours, however, had reached Dr Burney, who was informed that Mme de Staël's house in Paris had been a hotbed of revolution, and that her relationship with Narbonne was thoroughly improper. He had been advised that on no account should 'our Fanny' have 'the smallest connection with such an Adulterous Demoniac, much less intimacy'. The die-hard royalist *émigrés* in England were the principal source of such attacks. These royalist extremists were as much Germaine's bitter enemies as the revolutionary extremists, and equally determined to destroy her.

Miss Burney was convinced that her brilliant new friend must be the victim of calumny; 'but she is unfortunately so unguarded and so little governed by common rules, even those of France . . .'. Forced by her prejudiced family and friends to withdraw from Mme de Staël's society, she could not help feeling mortified. 'I wish the world would take more care of itself and less of its neighbours', observed Miss Burney who, unlike Germaine, was disinclined to take risks or flout the social conventions. Mme de Staël remained puzzled and rather resentful towards her. 'Is a woman treated as a minor all her life in this country?', she asked Susanna Phillips. 'It seems to me that your sister is like a girl of fourteen.'

At Juniper Hall, where Talleyrand (in exile in London) came to visit, Narbonne was feeling the strain of Germaine's presence. It was she who had encouraged him to play a leading role in public affairs, and who went on dreaming of him as the active leader of the moderate party. He, on the other hand, lacked perseverance: he was already weary of everything, and deeply shaken by the news of Louis XVI's execution. After all, to him Germaine was the latest of many, whereas she saw her lover as her 'tutelary god'. She felt convinced that she was in the grip of a 'grande passion' which necessarily overruled all the moral laws. Her sublime disregard for social convention bothered him. No breath of scandal, it will be noted, ever touched him in their liaison, such being the iniquity of the double standard. It was with some relief that Narbonne saw his energetic and demanding mistress aboard ship at Dover in May 1793, promising to rejoin her as soon as it was safe for him to travel to Switzerland.

Under the disapproving eye of her parents at Coppet — her mother finally refused to speak to her — Germaine waited desperately for Narbonne's letters, which were far from frequent. She remembered how her father used to write to her by daily courier whenever they were apart. To Narbonne she sent a detailed route that would enable him to avoid all the danger spots, and bought a house for him near Nyon. Narbonne made promises and invented pretexts for staying where he was. Extreme as her language had been in his praise, it became even more extravagant in her pain which, she said, would move Marat to pity. She reminded him of all she had done for him: how she had paid his debts, how she had saved his life. She reminded him of their sons, Auguste and Albert. She reminded him how she had risked everything, her reputation, her very existence, for his sake. She accused him of ingratitude, cruelty and indifference — all to no effect.

There is something disproportionate in her letters to Narbonne — and she knew it. They were being written at the same time as the Terror was raging in France and she was trying to save her friends from the guillotine. Yet the despair she felt and her dread of solitude were real, expressed in the agonizing cries of an abandoned Dido as she reproached the ungrateful Aeneas and mounted the funeral pyre. The bitterness she felt affected her health, her work. She had believed in the ideals of the Revolution, but it was being stained with blood. She had trusted in happiness and *gloire* with Narbonne, but he — like the frivolous product of the old regime he was — had failed her.

All her illusion and disillusion would go to fuel the book she was writing *On the Influence of the Passions*, where her own feelings are expressed in general terms. There, she wrote tellingly of woman's fate:

Nature and society have disinherited one half of mankind; strength, courage, genius, independence, all belongs to men . . . the laws of morality itself, according to the opinion of an unjust society, seem suspended in the relations between men and women; . . . they [men] can have received from a woman the favours, the tokens of devotion which would bind together two masculine friends, two companions in arms, and which would dishonour one of them if he were to prove capable of forgetting these; [yet] they can have received the same from a woman, and extricate themselves from everything . . .

She used almost the same words in her tale about a betrayed woman, *Zulma*, a work which, she said, 'more than any other belongs to my very soul . . .'.

While in the throes of rage, hope and despair about the date of Narbonne's putative arrival in Switzerland, Germaine encountered in June 1793 a Swedish exile who was living under an assumed name and whose attentions she at once reported to Narbonne. Count Adolph Ribbing had been exiled for his part in the assassination of Gustavus III, and despite her loathing for violence, Germaine did not appear to be repelled by the extremely handsome regicide. Indeed, she eventually acquired some of his republican views. It was with Ribbing that she found consolation.

At this time, the invalid Mme Necker was nearing her end. She sent for Germaine and reproached her once more for her association with Narbonne: 'I am dying of the grief your guilty and public liaison has caused me'. This was manifestly untrue, but it was enough to add to Germaine's sense of guilt at her mother's death in May 1794. By the end of July, Narbonne finally arrived at Mézeray, near Lausanne, where Mme de Staël was then living. Their affair was at an end. He renewed his liaison with Mathieu de Montmorency's mother, while Ribbing would ultimately disengage himself from Germaine and depart. Another was about to revive her dream of happiness in union with power.

5 Politics under the Directory

When Robespierre was toppled on 9 Thermidor (27 July) 1794, the blood from his broken jaw staining the document he was signing, France entered a period of anarchy. Prominent among the men who overthrew the Incorruptible was Tallien, who had escorted Mme de Staël to the Swiss frontier nearly two years before. At the time of this sudden reversal of fortune, which led the dictator she hated to the guillotine, Germaine was in Switzerland, dreaming of political activity. Far from idle, she was engaged in writing her study of the passions, together with her first important shorter political and literary works.

In September 1794, she was not at home when an extremely tall gentleman with striking red hair called on her. Determined to make her acquaintance, he galloped after her carriage. Soon, they were deep in conversation. At twenty-seven, just a few months older than she was herself, the ambitious Benjamin Constant had as yet accomplished nothing.

He came of a well-connected Swiss family, but had been brought up in the most eccentric way. His mother having died shortly after his birth, his father passed the boy around between a mistress of his and various female relatives, and then entrusted him to a series of unpromising tutors. These included one who proved to be a sadist; and another, an atheist, who chose to live in a brothel and who kept the boy with him there. Other equally shady pedagogues followed, not least an unfrocked monk who committed suicide. Nothing, however, could quell the passion for learning of their immensely precocious pupil, who came to combine profound erudition with lifelong fidelity to the bordello and the gaming table.

Constant's brilliant intelligence and versatility could match Germaine's own. As one who knew them both well was later to declare:

> You have not known Mme de Staël unless you have seen her with Benjamin Constant. He alone had the power, through an intellect equal to hers, to stimulate all her intelligence, to make

her greater through the contest between them, to arouse an eloquence, a profundity of spirit and thought which were never displayed in all their brilliance except opposite him, just as he too was never truly himself except at Coppet. . . .

By the time Constant began to pay court to Germaine, he had already had several love affairs — and would have many more during their association — being still involved with the embittered novelist, Mme de Charrière. He was also unhappily married to a lady from Brunswick (where he served as court chamberlain), and would shortly be divorced. Germaine at first rebuffed his advances: she was to remain in pursuit of the elusive Ribbing for some two more years. Besides, she felt more attracted to the frail, chivalrous François de Pange (close friend of the poet André Chénier, who perished in the Terror). However, the affections of M. de Pange were otherwise engaged.

It was François de Pange who printed the first edition of her remarkable essay, *Reflections on Peace addressed to Mr. Pitt and the French*, at the end of 1794. The Whig leader, Charles James Fox, borrowed from it in his great anti-war speech to Parliament on 24 May 1795. In this essay, she proclaimed her loathing for Robespierre and for the Terror. She went on to challenge the policy of Pitt and the Allies at war with France, who were under the dire influence of reactionary royalist *émigrés*, a policy which had only served the purpose of the fanatical Jacobins. The Allies should have promoted the moderates and should have been concerned with the restoration of true order and liberty in France. For one must 'go forward with one's era', not try to turn back the clock. Besides, the ruin of France would lead inevitably to the ruin of Europe as a whole. Let the French be allowed to choose their own government freely; let them establish a constitution that would 'reconcile the possible with the desirable', and would preserve the safety of property as well as of the individual. This document was, in effect, a manifesto of her own moderate views, aimed at the new leaders in Paris along with the government in London. Much that she was to write in the following years was directed to furthering her own ideal of the middle way as well as Constant's political career.

It is not known precisely when Benjamin Constant became Germaine's lover, but by the beginning of 1795 he was living at

Coppet. Their relationship would never be tranquil. Deeply introspective, an incomparable master of ruthless self-analysis, Constant was torn between admiration for Germaine's brilliant talents and the ties of affection and obligation that bound him to her on the one hand, and the yearning for peace and quiet with some ordinary undemanding woman on the other. This division, common to many of Germaine's masculine contemporaries, would provide an enduring theme in her fiction. Constant himself was not above staging a fake suicide with opium in order to impress her; and she, who already knew how to use the threat of suicide as a weapon, learned from him to employ opium to that end. Still, the violent emotional scenes in which they indulged at Coppet would not, apparently, interrupt the flow of her writings.

The most notable of her early works of literary criticism was an *Essay on Fiction*, published in the spring of 1795. In which direction should fiction move, after the dreadful revelation of human perversity offered by the Terror?, she wondered. Dismissing anything either far-fetched or purely historical, she stressed that novels must be modern and truth-seeming: they must depict our normal feelings. Admittedly, novel-writing did not as yet command the reputation it deserved, but (she urged) a good novel could provide marvellous insights into the human heart. Here, she prefigured Benjamin Constant's powerful novel of self-analysis, *Adolphe*. It was no longer sufficient to deal only with the subject of love, she maintained; other passions besides love should now be probed in the light of recent events, including ambition, pride, avarice, vanity. 'What beauties could not be found in the Lovelace of the ambitious!', she exclaimed, foreshadowing less her own novels than those of the nineteenth-century masters, Balzac and Stendhal, creators of Rastignac and Julien Sorel. It is no wonder that Goethe was so impressed with her essay that he translated it for his German readers.

In May 1795, Germaine arrived in Paris with Benjamin Constant and reopened her salon. This was made possible because, a month before, M. de Staël had been received and honoured by the National Convention, the Swedish government being the first to recognize the new regime. Paris was in an uproar. Germaine could not help seeing how famine and paper money had reduced the poorer class to a distressing state. In April, dissatisfied Jacobin demonstrators had invaded the National Convention to demand measures against food shortages. Riots were still going on. Some Jacobin *députés* were deported without trial, and the riots in the faubourg Saint-Antoine, the working-class quarter, were repressed. To her husband and to Ribbing, Germaine made no secret of her gratification at the triumph of the National Convention (accomplished by the alliance between the bourgeoisie and the army). Later, she would examine this action with a greater sense of nuance.

Her salon was one of the most brilliant of the day. Among her friends were leading moderates like the writer, Marie-Joseph Chénier (brother of the poet); influential *idéologues* like Cabanis and Destutt de Tracy; and noted members of the constitutional committee, including Sieyès and Boissy d'Anglas, who were engaged in framing the Constitution of Year III (1795), with whom she could discuss their proposals and suggest those of Constant and herself.

Meanwhile, Germaine had upset many of her old friends, the constitutional monarchists, by publishing in the press her faith in the Republic, 'because it has been made clear to me that, in the present circumstances, republican government alone can give peace and liberty in France'. Her frequent use of the phrase 'in the present circumstances' shows how she was trying to relate ideas to facts. In the summer of 1795 she produced her pamphlet, *Reflections on Internal Peace*, which reaffirmed her support for the Republic. In her view, France was torn between two forms of fanaticism: on the one hand, the uncontrollable mass, misled by a system of 'vulgar equality'; on the other, the royalist reactionaries. She made it quite plain, though, that she was opposed to the death penalty either for terrorists or for *émigrés* who fought against their country.

Her aim was the creation of a third party, which now took the form of an alliance between moderate republicans and constitutional monarchists. But how far was this possible? She knew it would not be easy. The very words 'freedom' and 'virtue' had become corrupted through being mouthed by those who destroyed these ideals. This made it difficult for genuine lovers of freedom to find a convincing language. In revolutionary times, too, fanaticism often bred success, whereas a moderate party could never inspire single-minded support. The extraordinary character of fanaticism, she wrote, was that it united 'the power of crime and the exaltation of virtue'. The fanatic 'does not believe he is guilty, publishes his deeds instead of concealing them; he has decided to lay down his own life for the cause, and this idea blinds him to the atrocity of sacrificing others'. His self-sacrifice allows him to keep the sense of virtue while committing terrible crimes. 'It is this contrast, this double energy which makes fanaticism the most awesome of all human forces . . .', she tellingly declared.

The only way to avoid a recurrence of the demagogical tyranny of Robespierre was to establish a republic based on the condition of property. This was because, she felt, property gave a sense of responsibility which the property-less did not have. True, those without property were the majority of the nation, and ideally, government should be for this majority. But they were not yet ready. Under an equitable republic, they would enjoy civil liberty; there would be no unfair taxation or unfair legal system to penalize them. Nor would there be any system of privileges — 'political right is not a privilege, since it can be attained by a modicum of property'.

Those who do physical labour cannot free themselves from the narrow circle of ideas imposed by their work, she thought. However, she urged, 'It is their physical existence which must be cared for; it is the means of acquiring property which must be multiplied around them . . .'. It seems clear from these words that, although she conceived an élitist republic, she also envisaged the eventual accession of the impoverished and as yet uneducated mass to political responsibility through social amelioration. Her concept of property as the 'central bond' of the moderate party was drawn from her father. It is curious that these words of hers were penned not long before the unsuccessful 'Conspiracy of Equals', led by 'Gracchus' Babeuf, the first attempt to set up a system of political communism in France.

Mme de Staël's position in Paris was extremely precarious. As tension mounted, she was under attack from both extremes, the royalists and the Jacobins. Already, in August 1795, Legendre, her former butcher, now a *député*, speaking in the National Convention, accused her of conspiring with royalist *émigrés*. Her own imprudence, her generous intercession on behalf of proscribed aristocrats, led many to suspect her of being in league with the royalists, despite all her republican declarations. As for the royalists themselves, they were naturally violently opposed to the constitution of Fructidor (August) 1795, since it was framed in such a way as to preserve a republican majority. She was in real danger, and left Paris for Mathieu de Montmorency's estate at Ormesson. A royalist *coup d'état* was foiled by Barras and by the army under the command of the rising General Bonaparte. The conspirators were captured or in flight. François de Pange and Benjamin Constant were arrested, but they were freed on Germaine's personal appeal to Barras. She herself, although she was staying in the country at the time of the abortive royalist *coup*, was sent into exile.

There was nothing for it but to return to Switzerland, where she devoted her time to finishing her book on the passions and collaborating with Benjamin Constant on his political writings. What she did not know — despite her new access to Barras, the man of the hour — was that the Directory was keeping her under discreet surveillance at Coppet. Not until the spring of the following year did she learn by chance that she was on the list of those to be immediately arrested if she ever returned to France. The pretext that she was not French, although she had been born in Paris, was already being used to persecute her.

Her husband finally managed to have the decree of exile rescinded, but she could not return to the Paris region until the end of December 1796, when she resided with Constant at the Abbey of Hérivaux, his newly-acquired estate, helping him with his political works. Not until May 1797 was she able to settle again in her beloved Paris. There, on 8 June, she gave birth to Albertine (presumed to be Constant's daughter). A visitor who called to offer congratulations found her talking volubly to fifteen people around her bed, and remarked sourly that there were plenty of servants to look after the new baby.

Once more she was in the thick of political manoeuvring, engaged with Constant and other leading moderates in founding the Club de Salm, and trying to revise the Constitution of 1795. Friends urgently appealed to her for help. From her former lover, Talleyrand, who had sought asylum in the United States after being expelled from England, she had received wild letters. 'If I stay a year, I shall die here', he wrote desperately to Germaine. She lost no time in busying herself on his behalf. Now, thanks to her (he wrote), he was able to return home. Back in Paris, Talleyrand borrowed a large sum of money from her which he soon exhausted. How was he to survive without some position? 'I shall blow out my brains', he assured her. Germaine took this suicide threat seriously. She hurried to see Barras, whom she had long been badgering on Talleyrand's account. In the end, Barras yielded. So it was largely through her that Talleyrand became Minister of Foreign Affairs. She launched on the road to profit and power the man who was to prove the most ungrateful of all her protégés.

Once again, the royalists were gathering strength, even acquiring a majority in the Assembly. In the royalist press, Mme de Staël came under savage attack, chiefly as a woman. She was 'born devoid of grace . . . her look brazen, her amorous leanings depraved', according to one royalist scribe. She was called 'prostitute', 'hermaphrodite', 'the most wretched female intriguer in Europe'. There seems little doubt that she knew about the projected *coup d'état* of 18 Fructidor (4 September) 1797, engineered by the Directory to put paid to royalist gains; she went into hiding the night before, watching the preparations when cannons were being moved through deserted streets to surround the legislative chamber. It appears that she was in favour of the *coup*, because she wanted to save the Republic. What she did not approve was the purge that began on the following day, when royalist *députés* were being imprisoned and executed, or else deported in cages to French Guiana. Among the victims were some of her friends. Hastening to intercede for them, she managed to save one from the firing-squad at the very last moment.

The invincible General Bonaparte, who had favoured the *coup d'état*, arrived in Paris. Mme de Staël met him for the first time at a reception given in his honour at Talleyrand's in December 1797. Bonaparte was then in his late twenties, flushed with the glamour of early success, but careful to stress at the time his simplicity, his love of solitude and of philosophy, his fondness for the poems of Ossian (the Scottish bard — invented by Macpherson — whom Mme de Staël and many of her contemporaries revered as a genuine poetic genius). Admiring letters which she is said to have sent to Bonaparte when he was in Italy, and to which he did not reply, have not survived. Whatever illusions she may have cherished concerning the republican admirer of Ossian, she did not really favour military intervention in political affairs except as an unavoidable necessity 'in the present circumstances', nor had she ever thought well of government by one man even when she was a child. Doubtless she wanted to impress the hero of the hour with her own genius, and hoped to draw him into her orbit.

If so, she certainly misjudged her man. For once, Germaine was at a loss for words, when Bonaparte told her how sorry he was to have missed seeing Necker at Coppet. The more often she met 'the most intrepid warrior' (as she called him), the more she felt intimidated. She actually found it difficult to breathe in his presence. When she heard him speak, she was struck by his 'superiority'.

Germaine watched at the ceremony when Bonaparte was received by the Directors in the courtyard of the Palais du Luxembourg. His modest dress contrasted with their finery. Talleyrand (who was to help Bonaparte to found the imperial dynasty) emphasized in his address the austere hero's devotion to the abstract sciences and his love of peace. In fact, Bonaparte had set his mind on conquering Egypt and, in order to do so, he needed funds. These he intended to obtain by invading Switzerland. Germaine tried to dissuade him: he listened patiently to her reasons during a tête-à-tête that lasted nearly an hour; then he changed the subject and discoursed on his taste for a quiet country life and the fine arts.

Germaine left Paris in January 1798 to join Necker at Coppet. Her father refused to leave his home. They could hear the cannons of the victorious French invaders. She grieved at the injustice of uniting Geneva — a free state even though ruled by an oligarchy — to France. Still, the annexation made Necker legally French. She took his petition to be struck off the list of *émigrés* to the Directory, which unanimously agreed to grant it. At the same time, she began negotiating with the Directory — in vain — for the return of the two million francs which Necker had deposited in Louis XVI's treasury.

It was during 1798–9 that she worked on her considerable pamphlet, *Concerning the Present Circumstances for Ending the French*

Revolution and the Principles which should establish the Republic in France. This pamphlet — which dealt with the state of the parties, the nature of public opinion, the importance of legality, the role of the press and of writers and intellectuals, her opposition to the military spirit — was never published in her lifetime. She must have realized that its publication would prove dangerous for her. The continuing fluctuations between the royalist and the Jacobin extremists, both of whom she attacked in the work, made her own situation vulnerable whenever either party threatened to gain the upper hand. Besides, she was afraid her views might damage Constant who was hoping (vainly) to be elected *député* for the Geneva area in 1799.

In July of that year, Mme de Staël was expelled by the Directory, which had never regarded her with any favour. The reasons were not far to seek. She had little in common with this assemblage of men largely on the make. As one member of her circle declared:

> She had no real influence. However liberal and republican her opinions, she could not appeal to such a government. Her aristocratic habits and inclinations, her eagerness to intervene in political affairs and talk about them indiscreetly, her theoretical, idealistic way of judging everything, her fondness for friends opposed to the regime, made her troublesome to the Directory . . . .

Consequently, Germaine was not too distressed when, at Coppet, she learned through Sieyès and Constant about the Directory's imminent demise.

She arrived in Paris on the evening of 18 Brumaire (9 November) 1799, when Bonaparte, having returned victorious from Egypt, overthrew the Directory and established the Consulate. The part played by the constitution-maker Sieyès led her and her friends for a moment to think that this was a victory for the moderates, though Necker advised caution. Moreover, she had moved Sieyès to appoint Benjamin Constant member of the Tribunate. Bonaparte's brothers, Lucien and Joseph, were often to be found in her drawing-room. It looked — for a very brief moment — as if the doors were opening for Mme de Staël.

6 The Sword and the Spirit

The years when Bonaparte was seeking to establish his power were those when Mme de Staël attained immense literary fame. What the First Consul wanted to hear was a hymn of praise from an admiring conformist, as he set himself to win over opponents or waverers by bribes of advancement and office. He presented himself as the embodiment of the Republic and republican virtue, while skilfully consolidating his personal power; and so he had no desire to hear talk of what constituted true liberty. The clash between Bonaparte and Germaine de Staël gradually assumes the form of an exemplary struggle between power and spiritual values. If it brought her a great deal of anguish, it also promoted her world reputation.

The day before Benjamin Constant was due to address the Tribunate, he warned Germaine that his speech would inevitably compromise her. She replied simply: 'One must follow one's beliefs'. Constant spoke out on 5 January 1800 in favour of free discussion and independence for the Assembly, 'without which there is merely servitude and silence, a silence that the whole of Europe would hear'. By five o'clock, Germaine had received ten letters from friends she had invited who were hurriedly making their excuses, and soon her drawing-room was three-quarters empty. Joseph Bonaparte called to convey his brother's displeasure: 'Why doesn't Mme de Staël cast in her lot with my government?', the First Consul had asked Joseph. 'What does she want? Payment of her father's deposit? . . . I shall consent. Well, what does she want?'. Germaine replied to Joseph: 'It is not a matter of what I want, but of what I think'.

In the spring of 1800, Mme de Staël published her influential study, *On Literature Considered in its Relations with Social Institutions*. She was not just wildly ambitious in her desire to illustrate her argument by examples drawn from many different areas of literature (including Greek and Latin, Italian, Spanish, German, English and French, up to her own day), she was profoundly original in attempting such a colossal feat. Her book was also new in the way it demonstrated how literature was intimately related to forms of government and society; and how it had developed through such civilizing forces as the rise of Christianity; or how a finer sensibility had evolved because of greater respect shown to women in particular ages and climes.

Building upon the insights of her predecessors in the Enlightenment, Mme de Staël was able to propose a new kind of literature, suited to a new kind of post-revolutionary society. This new idea of literature — inspired by her personal impressions and predilections, her esteem for advances made in the Middle Ages, and her enthusiasm for the northern mists and melancholy of Ossian or the tragedies of Shakespeare — would appeal to her successors in their own efforts to create something different and personal to themselves and their own world. This book helped writers to break free from imitating the imitations of Greco-Latin models.

There was no word against Bonaparte himself in the work. Yet she spoke there about the dangers of the military and authoritarian spirit. And she went so far as to state that 'the art of writing would also be a weapon, the word would also be an act . . . if tyranny saw itself under attack from everything that condemns it, [such as] generous indignation and inflexible reason'. She also observed how literature itself had changed radically during the eighteenth century: 'It is no longer solely an art, but a means; it becomes a weapon for the human spirit . . .'. Moreover, she stressed that 'what authority must fear most is the man who preserves his faculty of judgement'. None of this was likely to appeal to a person as imperious as Bonaparte.

At once she was attacked in the press. It was evident that she lacked the erudition to accomplish such a far-reaching work without errors and omissions which were soon pointed out by specialists. An egregious remark of hers — 'Finally, the Greeks, however astonishing they are, leave few regrets' — naturally offended classicists and aroused ridicule. Her praise of the civilizing merits of Protestantism, as compared with the Inquisition, inevitably upset Catholics. Chateaubriand, as yet little known, who was working on *The Genius of Christianity*, felt peeved to find that she had forestalled him in discussing the civilizing merits of the Christian religion, and criticized her with a certain elegant

55

malice. However, apart from the perfectly reasonable criticism of her ideas, there were also politically motivated attacks upon her. One of the most cruel of these was penned by Chateaubriand's friend, the critic Fontanes. He condemned her as a woman who was aiming to function outside her proper feminine sphere, and who as a consequence met with greater and well-deserved severity.

No amount of criticism or anti-feminine prejudice, though, could detract from the sensation caused by the book, and the total impression of brilliance left by its innovatory insights. After *On Literature* (which ran to a second and revised edition), Mme de Staël's salon was once again thronged with visitors.

Weary of liberal opposition, in January 1802 Bonaparte purged the Tribunate of the most vocal moderates, including Benjamin Constant and Marie-Joseph Chénier. Through his brothers, Lucien and Joseph, the First Consul took the opportunity to deliver a sharp warning to Mme de Staël: 'Advise her not to try to stand in my way, . . . otherwise, I shall break her, I shall crush her'. By this time, Germaine had no more illusions or doubts about Bonaparte's dictatorial intentions.

She expressed her indignation at the promulgation of the Concordat with Rome which reasserted papal authority over the French Church, and which upset many independent-minded republicans. Indeed, disapproval of the Concordat was one of the prime motives of the republican conspiracy led by Bonaparte's rival, General Moreau. Although Mme de Staël's friend, General Bernadotte, sympathized with this conspiracy, he was far more prudent than she, and managed to avoid being compromised. As for Bonaparte, he was utterly convinced that the author of *On Literature* was involved in the plot. The conspiracy was crushed; General Moreau was sent into exile; and the lesser fry were crowded into prison. Those who were eventually released did not dare to speak of the horrors they had seen.

That summer, shortly after Bonaparte declared himself Consul for Life, Necker published his *Final Views on Politics and Finance*, where he called for republican government, and denounced military power. Bonaparte was furious: he believed — mistakenly — that Mme de Staël had influenced her father. Germaine told a friend that Bonaparte 'fears me. That is my joy and my dread'. She foresaw proscription, felt ill at the thought of it: 'and yet I do not want any remedy that would be degrading'. The publication of her novel, *Delphine*, in December 1802, following upon Necker's objections to the new regime, exhausted Bonaparte's patience, and led to the very proscription she feared. He forbade her to stay in Paris. He must have known that, by exiling her from the capital and her friends, he was imposing the most exquisite mental punishment he could devise for her.

Delphine, although set in the recent past, in the revolutionary period 1790–2, alluded to many topical controversies, such as the merits and demerits of the Revolution and its consequences; the nature of true religious belief compared with destructive obscurantism (a theme of the moment because of the Concordat); the life-denying power of existing society and social conventions; the current attitude to marriage as a financial arrangement; and the need for divorce (the decree permitting divorce was passed in 1792, to be modified under Bonaparte). Written in a form still quite popular, that of letters, the novel allows the author the opportunity to convey the emotions and reactions of a number of women placed in widely different situations, whether spinsters, widows, happy or unhappy wives, whose destiny is governed by wealth or poverty, by beauty or the lack of it.

The generosity and imprudence of the heroine, Delphine, a young widow of independent means and of independent views on conduct, religion and politics — a highly idealized portrait of Germaine herself — make her the victim of calumny and prove the source of all her misfortunes. Delphine falls in love with Léonce de Mondoville, an irresistibly attractive nobleman who is ruled by the code of honour and by respect for public opinion. Their mutual passion is thwarted by their ill-assorted natures, and by the machinations of Delphine's false friend, Mme de Vernon, a woman with all the charm and machiavellism of Germaine's former lover, Talleyrand. Once Mme de Staël had incurred Bonaparte's displeasure, Talleyrand had dropped her with wounding alacrity. The novelist has the dying Mme de Vernon feel remorse for her betrayal, which has ruined the lives of Delphine and Léonce. This deathbed repentance appears as a form of literary revenge on the ungrateful Talleyrand, whom Germaine had helped to a position of power, and who was never to do anything to assist her when she was being persecuted by Bonaparte.

Many other aspects of the novel are drawn from Germaine's own experiences: for instance, the divergent expectations of the sexes; the painful effect of calumny; the scene where Delphine tries to save Léonce from execution under the Terror, a scene enacted by Germaine herself when attempting to rescue one of her friends. Extravagant as the novel may appear in its use of melodramatic plot devices, current among the novelists of her day, none the less it has moments of great power and psychological insight. Upon contemporary readers it made a profound impression. 'Do you know why nobody was at the theatre the day before yesterday?', inquired Roederer in the *Journal de Paris*. 'Why, to-day, Sunday, there will be few attending mass? . . . It is because the whole of Paris is behind closed doors reading Mme de Staël's new novel.'

Everything about *Delphine* was bound to annoy Bonaparte. Here is a heroine who relies on the dictates of her conscience alone. Besides, just when he was trying to win the support of the clergy, Mme de Staël revived religious controversy by having her mouthpiece, the liberal-minded Henri de Lebensei, portray Protestantism as the religion of liberty, and by showing Catholicism as a form of dark and gloomy enslavement. She condemned all those aristocrats who had voluntarily left the country at the Revolution (and had thus abandoned the king to his fate), just when Bonaparte was trying to win over the royalist *émigrés*. And, at a time when the First Consul aimed to establish social conformity and a moral veneer, here was the novelist discussing the hypocrisy of contemporary society, the misery of forced marriages, and the problem of divorce. Moreover, while he was contemplating renewed war with England, she was evoking the merits of English respect for the law.

In the press, attacks on the novelist's work were orchestrated by the government, many of them betraying sheer hatred of her as a woman. *Delphine* was even compared with the marquis de Sade's *Justine*: the heroine of her book and its creator were proclaimed immoral. The Irish novelist, Maria Edgeworth, who was among the visitors from the British Isles who flocked to France during the Peace of Amiens, observed that *Delphine* was being 'cried down' in the French circles she frequented. It was

58

also being warmly defended by Mme de Staël's friends and admirers.

Germaine could scarcely believe that the First Consul, once again at war with England, would find time to execute severe measures against herself, whom she liked to project as 'a weak woman'. In fact, Bonaparte had a mania for detail that was not confined to military matters. When, hoping to be able to slip back into Paris unnoticed, Mme de Staël moved to Maffliers, some twenty-eight kilometres from the capital, Bonaparte let her know that, if she remained there, she would be taken to the frontier by the police. Friends, including Joseph Bonaparte, interceded for her; she herself wrote a pathetic letter to the First Consul — in vain. On 15 October 1803 a polite officer called, with the order that, as a 'foreigner', she must leave 'within twenty-four hours', never to come closer to Paris than forty leagues, or about one hundred and sixty kilometres. Twenty-four hours' notice was sufficient for a conscript, Germaine told the officer indignantly, but not for a woman with three children. She persuaded him to allow her a few days in Paris to prepare for her departure and to take leave of her friends.

Where was she to go? The prospect of an obscure existence, somewhere in the French provinces, appalled her. Of course, she could always stay with her father at Coppet. Every parting from him was painful, with its underlying terror that this might be the last. All the same, life in Switzerland appeared to her too bland and boring. War now prevented her from reaching England. She decided that she would go to Germany and, on 28 October 1803, she set out for Metz with thirteen-year-old Auguste; Albertine, then aged six; and with Benjamin Constant as escort.

Why Germany? Her curiosity about the new movement of ideas in Germany had been growing for some years. Several of her cultivated Swiss friends had told her of the important intellectual and literary activity there. Benjamin Constant, who had studied at Erlangen and had lived in Brunswick, knew German well and talked of what he had read. She herself was well acquainted with a number of important works in translation, including Goethe's *Werther*. No less a person than the Prussian envoy to France, Wilhelm von Humboldt, had been teaching her his native language. At Metz, Germaine conversed with Charles de Villers, author of a scholarly study of Kant's philosophy, with whom she had been corresponding. At first, she contemplated using her visit to Germany to write a short introduction to German thought — a project that would eventually become far more ambitious in scope.

Germaine did not look forward to the journey, with its bad roads, uncomfortable inns, its difficulties and hazards. It seems unlikely that, without Bonaparte's persecution, she would have spent years travelling across Europe. For her, travel spelt a plunge into the unknown. To find herself in unfamiliar places, among indifferent strangers, exacerbated her sense of solitude, her feeling of being in limbo. She was therefore immensely grateful to Constant for accompanying her — the more so because their long relationship had remained what Constant called 'a continual storm or rather a complication of storms'. He himself had spent amatory interludes with less demanding women, while in the previous year Germaine had become briefly attached to Dr Robert Robertson (a Scot acting as travelling companion to the son of the Duke of Argyll).

That Benjamin Constant and Mme de Staël thought alike on many important matters did not necessarily always prove a bond. He could still complain about her in his diary:

> It is politics, a demanding love as at eighteen, the need for society, the need for *gloire*, melancholy as in a desert, the need for influence, the need to shine, everything contradictory and complicated . . . She unites the most outstanding qualities of mind and heart, but she sets all her friends on edge. What then will be the fate of the man on whom her life comes to rest? Her life that she wants to lead to suit herself and does not want to lead alone . . . .

And he added that 'since she captivated me, she has subdued me by the violence of her displays of suffering. I have not spent a day without being furious with her and with myself.' Frequently, however, Constant recognized Germaine's innumerable good qualities: 'There is nothing on earth as kind, as loving, as witty and devoted as she. And Albertine!', he was to confide to his diary.

In effect, their situation had entered a new phase, and a new

60

possibility had opened for Constant. In December 1800, Germaine and her husband had separated. Seventeen months later, M. de Staël, in total decline after having encompassed his own financial ruin, died as she was taking him back with her to care for him at Coppet. Germaine was now free to marry again. Many candid entries in Constant's diary reveal his vacillation: does he really want to marry her, or lead a quiet life with someone more amenable? As for Germaine, she had had quite enough of marriage with M. de Staël, and she did not know whether she wished to repeat the experience.

When Germaine crossed the German frontier with Constant and her children on a chill November day, she was not at all impressed by the inns, the food, the inhabitants or the talk. At Frankfort, she went to the theatre, to concerts and art galleries. Then, suddenly, Albertine fell ill with fever. Germaine was distraught, overcome with guilt, unable fully to comprehend the doctors. Fortunately, after a period of uncertainty, Albertine recovered, and the party left for Weimar. There, the whole picture changed for the better. The Grand Duke, his wife and his mother welcomed Necker's daughter warmly at court. Everyone had read *Delphine*. She met leading writers, including Wieland, 'the German Voltaire', and Schiller, creator of that lofty libertarian drama, *Don Carlos*; though Goethe tried (for as long as he could) to keep out of her formidable way.

The quiet, uneventful, meditative life of Weimar suddenly acquired an unexpected animation. Schiller said that Mme de Staël was 'the most combative, the most gesticulative' person he had ever seen, but he acknowledged that she was 'also the most cultivated and the most gifted'. It was exhausting to keep up with her. He wrote to Goethe: 'She insists on explaining everything, understanding everything, measuring everything. She admits of no Darkness; nothing Incommensurable; and where her torch throws no light, there nothing can exist'. This was not entirely fair. Germaine kept an open mind; for she not only wished to learn all she could herself, she now intended also to convey what she learned about German culture to the French. That was why she was always asking questions that tired Schiller and others. 'Here is a world of ideas absolutely new to me', she would write excitedly to Necker, telling him that she was planning a book about Germany. She persuaded various German scholars to collect information about their native literature for her, while a young Englishman, Henry Crabb Robinson (who was living in Germany in order to study the life, literature and thought of the country), gave her lessons in German philosophy.

Meanwhile, after having bombarded the mistrustful Goethe with letters, she finally met the great man when the Grand Duke persuaded him to return to Weimar. At Goethe's home, in tête-à-tête or in small gatherings of friends, they conversed mightily. But as soon as Goethe heard that she was proposing to publish his conversations with her, he became less forthcoming. All the same, his Olympian coolness had thawed sufficiently for him to write quite warmly to the composer Zelter in Berlin: ' . . . we have already had the good fortune to have Mme de Staël with us for a month. This extraordinary lady is soon leaving for Berlin, and I shall give her a letter for you. Go and see her at once; she is very easy to get on with. . .'.

If her reception by the great in Weimar gave her confidence, her stay in Berlin confirmed her fame. Benjamin Constant had parted from her in Leipzig — where they had exchanged a written promise to marry — and he had returned to Switzerland. She was alone to savour the gracious welcome of Queen Louise of Prussia, the invitations from the nobility, the encounters with noted men of letters, savants and philosophers. The story goes that on meeting Fichte, Germaine asked the philosopher to give her a brief summary of his concept of the ego, interrupting him delightedly after ten minutes: 'That is enough, Monsieur Fichte, I understand you perfectly'. As it happens, the subject of the empirical ego and the absolute ego served as a private joke between herself, Schiller and Goethe. It was in Berlin that she made the acquaintance of August Wilhelm Schlegel, the well-known translator of Shakespeare and Calderón, and founder (with his brother) of the *Athenäum*. Germaine saw how helpful Schlegel's deep learning could be to her, and she managed to engage him as her assistant and as tutor to her children.

Then, several members of the Prussian nobility called to tell her of bad news: her father was seriously ill. Her friends did not think that she should be told the worst at once. In fact, Necker was already dead. Constant, having just arrived back in Switzerland, at once set out again to rejoin Germaine. He met her at Weimar, and told her the truth. She collapsed in despair. In grief

View of Coppet in 1791

(*above*) Benjamin Constant
(*left*) Eric-Magnus, Baron de Staël, from a painting by
    Westmuller

Goethe in 1828, from a painting by Stieler

CORINNE

OU

L'ITALIE.

PAR MAD. DE STAËL HOLSTEIN.

. . . . Udrallo il bel paese,
Ch' Apennin parte, e 'l mar circonda; e l' Alpe.
PÉTRARQUE.

TOME PREMIER.

I

———————

PARIS,

A LA LIBRAIRIE STÉRÉOTYPE, chez H. NICOLLE,
rue des Petits-Augustins, n°. 15.
1807.

Title page of the first edition of *Corinne*

John Rocca, second husband of Mme de Staël

George Gordon, Lord Byron,
after a painting by George Sanders

Albertine de Staël

and guilt at her absence during her father's last illness, she cried: 'He was my brother, my friend, my husband, he was everything to me . . .'.

With Constant and Schlegel, Germaine travelled back to Coppet, arriving there on 19 May 1804. No sooner was she home than she busied herself with Necker's papers. She was to publish, a few months later, *Manuscripts of M. Necker*, together with her touching filial essay, *On the Character of M. Necker and his Private Life*. By this time, she had made up her mind that, after all, she would not marry Benjamin Constant.

In December 1804, shortly after Napoleon's coronation as emperor, the restless Germaine was again on the road, this time to Italy, with Schlegel in attendance. A freedom-loving Swiss scholar and member of her circle, Sismondi, who was working on his history of the Italian republics, was to join them *en route* at Turin. These two distinguished scholars would act as her intellectual guides in Italy. It was too soon, she knew, to write the book on Germany that she had in mind — far more research and reflection were needed — but she felt she could more readily develop the idea for a novel that had come to her when she was present at a play with music given in Weimar. This novel was to be *Corinne, or Italy*.

Still grieving for Necker, Germaine crossed the Alps to find Italy in the lugubrious grip of winter — an experience she gave to Lord Oswald Nelvil, the Scottish hero of her novel, deeply melancholy at the loss of his father and obsessed by filial guilt. Among the leading figures she met in Milan was the illustrious poet and patriot, Vincenzo Monti, who gradually helped to dispel some of her prejudices about his country. Her journey took her to Rome, and thence to Naples. She was intrepid enough to ascend Vesuvius, then only accessible by mule and on foot; and to visit temples at Báia by being carried over the swamps on the shoulders of sailors. In that age, there were not many ladies on the verge of thirty-nine whose keen curiosity would impel them to do as much. She saw Pompeii, and climbed Mount Miseno, which she was to make famous as the setting for Corinne's poetic meditation — a scene later depicted by the painter Baron Gérard with herself as Corinne.

It was on her return to Rome that Germaine's appreciation of Italy deepened. Wilhelm von Humboldt, now Prussian envoy in Rome, acted as her guide. Angelica Kauffmann, the Swiss artist who was also an accomplished musician, painted her portrait (unfortunately lost), and introduced her to the great neo-classical sculptor, Antonio Canova, whose studio Germaine visited. A young cosmopolitan Portuguese diplomat, Pedro de Souza, who chanced to be in mourning for his father, accompanied her on long walks among the ancient ruins and the grandiose monuments. His sympathetic presence endowed the Roman scene with a pleasurable melancholy, a twilight glow. Yet he responded to her advances with reserved delicacy, contriving to elude her pressing invitations. Her attachment to him would follow the usual course from passionate illusion to passionate disillusion.

The return journey took Germaine to Florence, where she could discuss the work of the dramatist, Alfieri, who had died not long since, with the Countess of Albany, his mistress of many years. Theirs seemed to Germaine to have been an ideal liaison of the sort that eluded her. In Venice, which was under Austrian domination, Germaine flirted with Count Maurice O'Donnell, a young Austrian officer of Irish descent. By the time she reached Milan, Napoleon had just been crowned king of Italy there.

As soon as Germaine returned to Coppet in the summer of 1805 she began work on *Corinne, or Italy*. She also held court. It was the beginning of the great years of Coppet, when many of the most gifted or influential figures in Europe were to call or stay, to discuss literature, politics and ideas, often far into the night. In this interchange, Germaine encouraged and stimulated her talented guests to produce some of their finest works. She entertained them in her private theatre, where she herself would perform as the rejected Hermione in Racine's *Andromaque*, or in plays that she wrote specifically for the stage at Coppet. It was at this time that Germaine embarked upon a liaison that was to last five years, with a young, handsome, elegant Swiss gentleman, Prosper de Barante, the future historian.

Even after all that Bonaparte had made clear to her, she still could not give up all hope of returning to Paris, where her son Auguste was studying to enter the Ecole Polytechnique. In April 1806, she ventured to settle at Auxerre, much to local astonishment at the presence of the celebrated and controversial authoress. Then she moved rather nearer to Paris, at Rouen, though even the company of Constant and Schlegel could not entirely relieve for her the tedium of provincial life. Besides, Constant was breaking free. Well before she became involved with young Prosper de Barante, Constant had renewed his attachment to Mme du Tertre, a lady he had known years before in Brunswick as Charlotte von Hardenberg. He was still with Germaine, however, when she stayed just north of Paris, near Meulan, to finish *Corinne* and correct the proofs.

Napoleon, campaigning in Prussia, and informed by his spies of Mme de Staël's slightest movements, told his Minister of Police, Joseph Fouché, one-time instrument of the Terror, to enforce the forty-league limit on 'this hussy', 'this real bird of ill omen', 'this whore and a dirty one into the bargain'. Germaine contrived none the less to slip into Paris for a few days in April 1807, before returning to Coppet. In hiding during the day, she only dared to venture forth at night, for a moonlight stroll along the *quais* she loved. It was a characteristic act of bravado.

The publication of *Corinne* in May 1807 proved an immense success, and thenceforward Mme de Staël was called by her heroine's name. The lovely Corinne, an orphan, born of a British father and an Italian mother, amazes everyone as an independent woman so gifted that she excels as poet and tragic actress, and is also remarkably skilled with the pencil and the lyre. When Corinne is being crowned at the Capitol in Rome, she is seen and admired by Lord Oswald Nelvil, a young man haunted by remorse at having failed his dying father. They fall in love as, in a reversal of roles, Corinne guides Oswald through the monuments, the art, the culture and society of Italy. A mystery surrounds her. Eventually, we learn that Corinne's father and Lord Nelvil's had been friends, and that she had once been destined for Oswald. But then Oswald's father, on observing her talents, had preferred Corinne's half-sister, the beautiful, modest Lucile, as a more suitable wife for his absent son.

On learning this secret, the guilt-ridden Oswald gradually withdraws. The suffering Corinne nobly finds an indirect way to release him from his promise to her. He marries Lucile, but they are not happy. Later, he returns to Italy with Lucile and their child, to find Corinne dying of her unrequited passion for him. Corinne refuses to see him. The book ends with the author's unrelenting comment: 'Did he forgive himself for his past conduct? . . . was he satisfied with a common fate after what he had lost? I do not know; in this regard I do not wish to blame or absolve him'. *Corinne* is the story of the genius who — like her creator — cannot find rest or happiness in contemporary society (a theme that was to become vital for writers in the Romantic mode). But one original aspect of the novel is that this particular genius is a woman. The book also conveys the author's ideas on the contrast and conflict in outlook between northern and southern Europe, embodied in her principal characters; her views on beauty, art, literature and the state of Italy. All this appealed greatly to those who either knew or who more probably yearned to visit the country.

At first glance, there seems to be nothing political about *Corinne*. Napoleon did not see the novel in that light. The Corsican victor of Marengo, the newly-crowned king of Italy, noticed at once that his name and his exploits were conspicuous by their absence. And this at a time when the emperor was accustomed to hear in adulatory addresses such words as 'Napoleon stands above human history. He stands above admiration; our love alone can rise to his level'. Indeed, his blood-stained victories were obliquely condemned in the novel, for when Corinne is crowned at the Capitol, 'her victorious chariot had cost nobody any tears . . .'. The decline into which once glorious Italy and the Italians had fallen, was ascribed by Mme de Staël to the absence of liberty and independence and, by inference, to foreign conquest and occupation. *Corinne*, by noting every possible sign of reawakening, encouraged faith in a forthcoming Italian renaissance. In this way, the book strengthened Italian national consciousness, and helped to stimulate a movement that would ultimately lead to the unification of Italy.

It is scarcely surprising that when Auguste, then only seventeen, was received by the emperor at Chambéry in December 1807, and asked for his mother to be allowed to return to Paris, where she would confine herself to literature, he met with short shrift. 'Tell your mother my mind is made up. As long as I live she will never set foot in Paris again.' Besides, Napoleon added sharply, 'You can make politics by talking literature, morality, fine arts, anything you like. Women should stick to knitting'.

Why was Napoleon so strict with Mme de Staël? If he did not put her in prison, along with so many others, it was because he knew perfectly well — as he told Auguste — that there would be an outcry in favour of the celebrated writer, and that such an act would do him more harm than good. He knew also that she could not possibly stop discussing everything, whereas he demanded not only absolute respect for his authority but the quiet 'order' which made a great deal of the literature of the imperial era in general so mediocre. The high-minded Chateaubriand could resign his post and could pen memorable phrases of impassioned indignation, when Napoleon had the young duc d'Enghien seized on foreign territory, brought back to France, and shot. But Chateaubriand did not suffer any punishment for his protest, presumably because, unlike Mme de Staël, he was not in active independent opposition all the time; nor was he in constant contact with a host of notabilities and opinion-makers in the country and throughout Europe. Napoleon moved against the author of *Corinne* because he saw her as a dangerous enemy of his policies. There seemed to be no prospect that he would relent.

7 Persecution, Triumph and Tragedy

At first, Germaine seemed almost unaware of how provocative her candid political talk and her actions must appear to Napoleon. Later, in proud and active defiance, she would begin to work against him, his constant wars and his near-successful attempt to dominate Europe. As with all her campaigns, she did not quite realize what the consequences of her actions would be. All the same, Napoleon's persecution of Mme de Staël was to lead her into an epic adventure, the most astounding one to be undertaken by a woman in that age.

While Auguste was trying to persuade the emperor to relent, his mother was in Vienna, where she spent a brilliant five months. There, under constant surveillance by French and Austrian police, she talked with the leading figures of the day, and pursued an affair with young Count Maurice O'Donnell, whom she had first encountered some two and a half years before in Venice. It was in May and June 1808 that she had two meetings with Friedrich Gentz, close collaborator of Metternich, and one of Napoleon's greatest enemies. Gentz found her 'indubitably great'. His first impression was that 'one could talk to her forever'. Napoleon's reaction on learning of this encounter was forthright: 'You will let it be known', he told Fouché, his Minister of Police, 'that up to now she has been seen as a crazy woman, but that now she begins to join a set opposed to public order'. The emperor believed that she remained afterwards in close contact with Gentz, though this was not the case, and he responded accordingly.

Meanwhile, Mme de Staël devoted the next two years to finishing her book about Germany and German culture. By April 1810, her publisher was setting the book in print, while she stayed at the grandiose château de Chaumont on the Loire, and then at the château de Fossé, enjoying the company of friends and correcting the proofs. Control over the written word in France had become more strict, after the creation of a new censorship office at the beginning of the year. Then, in June, Fouché, who had been relatively considerate to Mme de Staël, was replaced as Minister of Police by the far less indulgent General Savary, duc de Rovigo. The unsuspecting publisher had been submitting each section of the work to the censor, who asked for corrections to the first volume but passed the second, so that when the blow fell it was all the more savage.

Rovigo gave the order that she was to leave within twenty-four hours, and that all her manuscripts and proofs were to be confiscated. Appeals to the emperor proved vain. Indeed, Napoleon had personally decided to prohibit the book. 'Do you think, sir', said Rovigo to Germaine's messenger, young Auguste, 'that we have been fighting the Germans for eighteen years so that a person as celebrated as your mother can publish a book without mentioning us?' In October, *On Germany*, the result of six years' labour, was pulped.

Certainly, there was much in the work to annoy the emperor. Above all, he could not have been pleased by the tone of the book, where Germany, a defeated country thoroughly disdained by the French, was presented as one that had a great deal to offer its conquerors. Throughout, the emphasis was libertarian in spirit. If she discussed Goethe's *Egmont*, which centred on the sixteenth-century uprising in the Low Countries against Spanish domination, it was not difficult to see that what she had in mind was the revolt in the Tyrol or the resistance to Napoleon's forces in Spain. Men endowed with absolute power and who abuse it (like Attila the Hun) are shown to bequeath nothing but dust. The censor demanded the removal of passages which alluded to the impermanent legacy of absolute rulers. As for the atrophied state of literature during Napoleon's reign, she wrote: 'Good taste in literature is, in some respects, like order under despotism: it is vital to look into the price paid for it'. Morality should be the guiding star of governments: that was the gist of the unsought advice she proffered to the great adventurer who believed only in his own star.

The authorities were anxious to gain possession of the manuscripts and proofs of *On Germany* in case Germaine should have the book published abroad. In effect, she had managed to conceal her papers. One set of proofs was to be carried to safety in Vienna by Schlegel; while the other remained hidden in her own keeping and would finally be published in London in 1813. She was to have her immortal revenge then by including in the preface Rovigo's letter to her in its entirety, a perfect example of base and stupid officialdom. 'It seemed to me', wrote Rovigo, 'that the air of this country did not suit you, and we are not yet reduced to seeking models among the peoples you admire. Your last work is not French.' And he added a postscript forbidding her to leave the country by the Channel ports, and thus to take refuge in England. Germaine had acquired a passport for the United States (where Necker had bought property), and she had often toyed with the idea of going there. Instead, she withdrew, shattered, to Coppet.

There was one consolation: her meeting with John Rocca, last in the line of handsome young men who at intervals had briefly renewed her youth. Rocca, Geneva born, an officer in the hussars who had been gravely wounded in the fighting in Spain, was already suffering from consumption. He was twenty-three, Mme de Staël forty-five. The difference between Rocca and many of his youthful predecessors was that he was really deeply devoted to Germaine, and seriously wished to marry her. For her part, she was not at all keen to give up the title of baroness and the name she had made famous. All the same, she and Rocca exchanged a promise to marry, a formal promise in the presence of a Protestant pastor.

As for Benjamin Constant, three years before this solemn engagement, he had secretly married the long-suffering Charlotte von Hardenberg, but he could not bring himself to inform Mme de Staël of the fact. It was Charlotte who eventually revealed all to Germaine. Somehow, the author of *Corinne* persuaded the couple not to make their union public. Frequently leaving his luckless wife to her own devices, Constant continued to be found in Germaine's company. This tangle was ultimately untied by the advent of John Rocca and, above all, by the force of circumstances which carried Germaine away from Constant's orbit.

Ever increasingly, Mme de Staël was made to feel a prisoner at Coppet. She was not permitted to move beyond Geneva. The newly-appointed *préfet* carried out his orders to the letter, so that when she travelled with her family to take the waters at Aix-les-

Bains, she was forced to return home. Her old friend Mathieu de Montmorency came to visit her, and was sent into exile; and so was her close confidante, that great beauty, Juliette Récamier, who insisted on coming to Coppet to see her. Both Montmorency and Mme Récamier were also involved with opponents of the regime, but Germaine felt that they owed their exile in large part to their fidelity to her, and she was deeply distressed. Other friends of hers were warned by the *préfet* to stay away. Some were so afraid that they kept aloof of their own free will.

The sense of isolation, the feeling that her situation was harmful to her sons and her daughter, the dread possibility that she might end in prison (along with the English civilians and the Spanish prisoners of war who had been languishing in captivity for years) — all this forced Germaine to think seriously about escape. Schlegel was the prime mover, and he quietly began to make preparations. Germaine could not leave at once, for she was supposedly suffering from dropsy. In actuality, she was pregnant by Rocca. On 7 April 1812, she gave birth to a son, Louis-Alphonse, in great secrecy — a secret that was soon known to the emperor. Fortunately, nobody knew about the arrangements for her flight.

After entrusting 'Little Us', as she and Rocca called their son, to a village pastor, and solemnly taking leave at her father's tomb in the grounds at Coppet, Germaine set out in her carriage on the afternoon of 23 May 1812, with her fan in her hand, as if she were just going for a short drive. Albertine was with her; Auguste and Rocca rode alongside. Albert left later on with the servants and her travelling coach. Outside Berne, Schlegel joined her. Leaving Auguste to return to Coppet, Germaine proceeded to Vienna, where she was well received. Still, the welcome was somewhat less warm than it had been four years earlier, for defeated Austria was now allied to France. In Vienna, she waited anxiously for passports for Russia, slow to arrive.

Two days after she left Vienna without them, Napoleon's invading armies crossed the River Niemen into Russia. After travelling across Bohemia, Moravia and Poland, Germaine and her party arrived at the Russian frontier at Brody, having been constantly harassed by the zealous Austrian police along the way. Her goal was St Petersburg but, because of the fighting around the direct route and her fear of being captured by the

French army, she had to make a very large detour by way of Kiev, Tula and Moscow.

Travelling conditions in a remote country at war — the long wait for horses, the primitive inns, the lack of what she called 'English comforts' — were far from easy. But she was quite astonished to discover that, even though the French army was advancing deep into Russia, she and her French-speaking party were received everywhere with generous hospitality. A keen observer, she found her imagination was stimulated by strange customs and new sights — the houses of Kiev that looked like a Tartar encampment from a distance; the sparse villages, the plains and birch forests on the monotonous road from Kiev to Moscow. 'It seemed to me that this country was the image of infinite space', she declared, 'and that eternity was needed to traverse it'. The third estate, so necessary for progress and literature and art (she commented), did not exist in Russia. Much as she disliked serfdom, she could not help noticing the close attachment between the nobles and the people. And she was moved by the resignation of the Russians, their acceptance of huge sacrifices, and the energy of their resistance to the French invaders.

The partly oriental splendours and extravagance of Moscow dazzled her, and she described them lyrically in her *Ten Years of Exile*, doubtless in order to give more pathetic weight to that city's destruction, which took place not long after her departure. Count Rostopchin, former Minister of Foreign Affairs, called on her and invited her to dine with him. When the French army was at the gates, he was to set fire to his great house, where she had been royally entertained. Mme de Staël was one of the last visitors from western Europe to describe the city as it looked before the inhabitants defied Napoleon by putting it to the torch.

Arriving in St Petersburg, she thanked heaven to see 'the English flag, signal of liberty, flying on the Neva'. Invitations flowed from nobles, ministers, court dignitaries. She encountered the elderly General Kutuzov, soon to be the architect of Napoleon's retreat from Moscow. Young Tsar Alexander I himself discussed grave matters with her as an equal, in what she called the manner of an English statesman rather than a sovereign. The Tsar even told her what Napoleon had said to him on the raft at Tilsit. He also informed her how he intended to improve the condition of the serfs. Mme de Staël saw him for the second time on his return from Finland, where he had gone to meet her old friend Bernadotte, now crown prince and effective ruler of Sweden, and where the two potentates had vowed never to make peace with Napoleon. In St Petersburg, she talked with notable English and German diplomats engaged in the struggle to defeat the usurper, and it was there that she began to formulate her own plan of campaign and to perceive her own role in the battle to destroy the emperor.

From St Petersburg, Mme de Staël travelled to Stockholm, where she arrived on 24 September 1812, and where she was warmly greeted by her friend Bernadotte. As she saw it, the opposition to Napoleon needed an outstanding military leader governed by enlightened principles and sincere liberal convictions. Germaine now tried to persuade everyone, including Bernadotte himself, that he was the desired moral leader; that he should take command of the anti-imperial alliance; and that he should govern France after the fall of the empire.

The struggle was a moral one, she insisted. If Napoleon were victorious, freedom and independence would disappear from Europe. 'Freedom is nothing but morality in politics', she declared. 'There are only two kinds of men on this earth', she maintained, 'those who serve tyranny and those who know how to hate it'. After victory, and the liberation of the countries occupied by Napoleon, there must be no return to the old order, but the regeneration of Europe. Every liberated country must enjoy constitutional liberties. She was proposing a definite policy based on her own political ideas.

Her eight-month stay in Sweden was marked by her propaganda effort on behalf of Bernadotte as the liberal hero of the age who, unlike Bonaparte, united genius with virtue. This was the gist of what she was writing to the crowned heads, leading politicians, generals, influential aristocrats she knew throughout Europe. At all hours, she was seen visiting Bernadotte who (it was reported) told her everything and even consulted her. His position was delicate, though, because much as he wanted the French throne, he had first to consolidate his position in Sweden. Moreover, as she well knew, Bernadotte lacked resolution, and so she tried to inspire him with her own enthusiasm. Besides all this political activity, Mme de Staël published in Sweden her *Reflections on Suicide*, where she retracted her earlier views on self-destruction. She also continued to work on *Ten Years of Exile*, and began writing *Considerations on the Principal Events of the French Revolution*, works of enduring significance, both of which were to remain unfinished and to be published posthumously.

Leaving Schlegel, now appointed Bernadotte's secretary, in Stockholm, Mme de Staël embarked for London on 9 June 1813, with Albertine and with Auguste, who had recently come to join his mother. Rocca served as their discreet escort. As for Albert, ever rash and difficult to control, he had joined the Swedish army. A few weeks after his mother's arrival in London, he was to be killed in a duel in Germany. It was a grievous blow.

In England, where she remained for nearly eleven months, Germaine would serve as Bernadotte's agent, criticizing Tory ministers for favouring the restoration of the Bourbons, and seeking support for Bernadotte's candidacy.

Arriving in Regency London, Mme de Staël was the celebrity of the hour, not only as the author of *Corinne* but as the most outspoken victim and opponent of Napoleon in Europe. Leaders of high society flocked to call on her at her hotel and to invite her to their homes. Among them was Lord Darnley, who entertained her at his Elizabethan mansion, Cobham Hall, in Kent, where Lord Erskine, the Lord Chancellor, discoursed for her benefit on the English penal code. Contact was made with Lord Grey, opposition leader in the House of Lords (whom she came to esteem as the perfect English gentleman), and with other prominent Whigs like Lord Holland and Samuel Whitbread. Among the poets, she made the acquaintance of Southey and Coleridge as well as Byron. Work was not forgotten, though. She negotiated with John Murray, Byron's publisher, a contract for *On Germany*.

By August, the nobility having departed according to custom for their country estates, London was virtually deserted. Mme de Staël spent much of August and September quietly in a rented retreat at Richmond (then a small town outside London), close by her friend, Elizabeth, Duchess of Devonshire, with whom she had corresponded for many years. In the autumn, Lord Lansdowne, the prominent moderate Whig, invited her to Bowood, his grand mansion in Wiltshire, where she entertained the company with poetry readings and dramatic performances. She conversed there with the brilliant polymath, Sir James Mackintosh, who became known as a great friend of hers, and with the noted parliamentarian, Sir Samuel Romilly, advocate of penal reform, Catholic emancipation and the abolition of the slave trade. She would become a keen collaborator of the leading abolitionist, William Wilberforce.

The publication of *On Germany* in November followed closely upon Napoleon's defeat at Leipzig and Germaine's renewed efforts for Bernadotte. Her book was received with great acclaim. Byron delighted in it, reading it 'again and again'. He realized that whatever faults it might have were far outweighed by its usefulness, its contribution to an appreciation of the literary and cultural ferment in Germany. Naturally, German critics tended to be more severe about omissions and flaws in a work which attempted to embrace the whole range of their literature, philosophy, religion and social mores. Yet no less a person than Goethe felt that the book's shortcomings could not make one forget what was fine and true in it. Here was a book which made people think, he said, and which gave a higher opinion of Germany than that held by Germans themselves. In short, Mme de Staël's great merit lay in putting Germany on the cultural map. Her idealistic view of the country was largely to prevail in France for nearly sixty years, until the Prussian invaders of 1870 shattered it.

All did not run perfectly smoothly for Mme de Staël in England, however. Her behaviour was a gift to the wags. Her gowns, thought to be excessively low-cut for her years, aroused amused comment. Once, at dinner, when a bone in her corset shot upwards, she struggled in vain to push it down, then called a manservant to remove it, while remaining blissfully unaware that she had offended English propriety. Her passion for talking volumes (as Byron observed) disturbed the more reticent British gentry. The eccentrically taciturn Duke of Marlborough, subjected in private to a long monologue, was forced to utter at last: 'Let me out!'.

Mme de Staël's lack of tact, her (understandable) disinclination to abide by such tedious customs as the withdrawal of the ladies in order to leave the gentlemen to their port and conversation after dinner, upset the sticklers for strict feminine etiquette.

Jane Austen, apparently, did not wish to meet her. Dandies like Beau Brummell amused themselves by playing hoaxes on her, though she did not always seem to realize that she was their butt. Even Byron, who recognized the stature of this 'fine creature, with great talents, and many noble qualities', could not resist teasing her. He wickedly insisted to her face that he found *Corinne* immoral because she had made all its virtuous characters dull and commonplace. In vain she tried to interrupt his determined eloquence on this theme: 'Quelle idée!' 'Mon Dieu!' 'Ecoutez donc!' 'Vous m'impatientez!' The irony of being reproved for immorality by so notorious a rake as Byron was not lost on her, and only increased his amusement.

There were graver disagreements. Many of the enlightened gentlemen with whom she conversed were followers of the utilitarian philosophy of Bentham, which she had long opposed. Some of her hosts tried to demonstrate to her that all was far from perfect in Regency England, pointing to such abuses as press-gangs and rotten boroughs. She came to realize for herself that there were flaws in English society, but at the same time much that she learned from British humanitarian reformers would pass into the last section of the *Considerations*, devoted to proposing the English constitution as a model for the French. What flaws there were seemed to her to be relative. When Sir Humphry Davy (inventor of the miners' safety lamp) complained that England was losing its sense of civic liberties, she retorted: 'And you count as nothing the freedom to say all that, and even in front of the servants!'

The fact that the Whigs were divided, and that one group of liberals persisted in warmly admiring Napoleon, puzzled and irritated her. It seemed inconceivable that the liberal-minded should be dazzled by the tyrant's power. As for the libertarian Byron, fascinated by Bonaparte, with the everlasting British insouciance of those who lack real experience of tyranny in action, he could not really 'believe that Napoleon was acquainted with all the petty persecutions that she used to be so garrulous about, or that he deemed her of sufficient importance to be dangerous'. Byron died too soon to read Napoleon's official correspondence, or the emperor's conversation as reported in the memoirs of his close adherents.

As the London season revived in the winter of 1813/14, Mme

de Staël frequently went to the theatre. She who, as a child, had admired Garrick, now saw the great Romantic actor Edmund Kean in Shakespeare. Lord Spencer invited her to Althorp, Lord Salisbury entertained her at Hatfield House. Amid the round of social pleasures, it was eventually becoming clear to her, however, that the cause of Bernadotte, for which she had fought so hard, was being lost, partly through his own vacillation. The Bourbons began to make approaches to her. Neither they nor their entourage had changed, she wrote to Benjamin Constant, but she saw she would have to submit. 'Don't you feel the wind of counter-revolution which . . . will soon overturn everything in France?', she asked her former companion.

With the increasingly successful Allied invasion of France, Mme de Staël felt deeply torn between her desire for Napoleon's downfall and her horror at French humiliation. She had not foreseen that the two would be interconnected. Provoked by Constant, she replied with an impassioned letter where her ambivalent feelings of reluctant admiration for the military genius and loathing for the despot are manifest. 'Forty battles are also a form of nobility — I hate the man, but I blame events which force me to wish him success — Do you want France to be trodden underfoot?', she cried in anguish, vowing to 'do nothing against France'.

After Napoleon's abdication at Fontainebleau on 6 April 1814, Mme de Staël was at last free to return to France. To her great sorrow, she found the outskirts of Paris and her beloved native city itself occupied by German and Russian troops. Her return from exile was a sort of personal triumph for her, but it was not the triumph of Bernadotte, of reconciliation and of moderate liberal ideas that she had planned. Without any great enthusiasm she supported the Bourbon regime and was received at court.

Those who read Napoleon's downfall as her victory — Tsar Alexander I; survivors of innumerable governments like Talleyrand and Fouché; victorious generals — thronged her drawing-room. The Duke of Wellington, whom she met for the first time in June 1814, was among them. Soon, she was keenly involved in activity for the abolition of Negro slavery. She took a great interest, too, in the preparations for the new constitutional Charter, and was present when it was promulgated by Louis XVIII on 4 June, though she was well aware of its shortcomings. To her, French society in 1814 resembled all too closely that of 1780: here once again were the haughty aristocrats and the clerics who sought and acquired political influence.

Having spent the summer of 1814 at Coppet, where she entertained many of her English friends, Mme de Staël returned to Paris for the winter. It was in March 1815 that she heard the astonishing news: Napoleon had escaped from Elba, had landed at Golfe Juan, and was rapidly advancing on the capital. Louis XVIII and his government fled. The historian Villemain, who saw the creator of *Corinne* at this time, remarked on the change in her. She was no longer her usual animated self, but seemed to be 'consumed by sorrow'. A number of leading Bonapartists approached her, urging her to remain in Paris. But she did not trust Napoleon's promises. Telling Villemain that the emperor 'will never have me on my knees', she departed hastily for Coppet.

During the Hundred Days, Napoleon found it expedient to present himself as the apostle of liberalism, and even did his best to win Mme de Staël to his side. Indeed, while he was in exile on Elba, she had learned of a plot against his life, and had informed his brother Joseph. Napoleon let her know that he was aware of 'how generous she had been towards him in his misfortune'. As for Benjamin Constant, after rashly excoriating the Corsican usurper just before Louis XVIII's flight, he was now helping Napoleon in his liberal pretentions, by drafting 'the Additional Act to the Constitutions of the Empire'. This constitution, familiarly known as *la benjamine*, led many of Napoleon's former opponents — including La Fayette — who dreaded the return of the Bourbons or who feared another Allied invasion, to choose what they considered the lesser evil and to rally to the emperor's cause with its new liberal veneer. Mme de Staël herself hesitated. What if Napoleon had returned for good? She would conceal this hesitation in her *Considerations* by condemning those libertarians (and, by implication, Constant) who deceived themselves about the emperor's true colours.

After the Allied victory at Waterloo and Napoleon's second abdication in June 1815, there was nothing for it but to renew her allegiance to Louis XVIII. If the regime was marked by the White Terror and by the ever-growing influence of reactionaries, it also restored to her the famous two millions that Necker had lent to the Royal Treasury. The need for this sum had become more pressing, not merely to repair her own fortune, depleted in the years of exile, but principally to provide a suitable dowry to enable Albertine to marry an impoverished nobleman, Victor, duc de Broglie. Worried about finding this dowry, Germaine had applied to Constant for the return of large sums that she, together with her father, had lent him in the past, promised amounts which he had no intention of restoring to this 'harpy'. The repayment of Necker's loan to the Royal Treasury put an end to the altercation with Constant.

At last, the betrothal of Albertine to Victor de Broglie (who was to become one of France's leading liberal politicians) could take place. In September, Germaine left with Albertine, Schlegel and Rocca (who was gravely ill), for Italy, where they spent the winter. In Pisa, in February 1816, Mme de Staël was gratified to see her daughter married to Victor de Broglie in two religious ceremonies, one Catholic and one Protestant.

At Coppet during the summer and autumn of 1816, Germaine welcomed many distinguished European writers, thinkers and politicians. News of their presence 'in the illustrious woman's salon' reached Stendhal: 'I am told that this autumn, on the shores of the lake, the most astonishing gathering took place: it was the States General of European thought . . . Voltaire never had anything like it'. Among the men of letters and title was Byron, in headlong flight from England — whither he was never to return — after the scandalous collapse of his marriage. At that moment, no one in good society wanted to receive the outcast. He was deeply touched, therefore, when Mme de Staël welcomed him warmly and even did her best — though without success — to effect a reconciliation with his wife.

That autumn, Germaine married John Rocca, in secret, at Coppet. Six days later, she set off with her young husband for Paris.

Her chief effort was now concentrated on attempting to bring about a reduction in the number of foreign troops on French soil and in the amount of France's debt to the Allies. She discussed these matters with the British ambassador, with George Canning when he passed through Paris. Above all, she succeeded in converting the Duke of Wellington to her views, pointing out to him all the ills caused by the military occupation. At the same time, she was busy revising the *Considerations*, and receiving in her salon the gifted men who were to be the principal liberal thinkers and politicians of the coming age.

The years of intense activity, the extreme emotionalism, the late and difficult pregnancy, the acute worry and tension of the long years of persecution and exile, the abuse of opium and other drugs to relieve insomnia — all these had left their mark on her physical appearance and condition. As she was leaving a reception given by Decazes, the king's favourite, on 21 February 1817, Mme de Staël suffered a stroke. Although she regained her powers of speech, she remained paralysed: 'I have been on my back for the last ninety days just like a tortoise, but with much more imagination than that animal . . . . It is a real punishment from heaven when the most active person becomes so to speak petrified. Yet I am not petrified in either mind or heart'. With her father's portrait before her, with the invalid Rocca and her family around her, she was visited by the Duke of Wellington, by Chateaubriand and Mme Récamier, and by many of her friends. Only Constant whose presence, it was felt, might disturb her, was not admitted.

After several months of acute physical suffering, Mme de Staël died in her sleep on 14 July 1817. She was fifty-one. Henceforward she belonged to posterity and to the history of liberty.

8   The Claim to Fame

The Writer

Mme de Staël's place and rank are not simple to assess, because she ventured into so many different fields. She was above all what the French call a *moraliste*, an analyst of human behaviour and attitudes; but she was also a student and historian of society, culture and ideas; a political thinker and activist; a literary critic; a novelist as well as the author of stories, plays and poems. Nor should it be forgotten that she wrote hundreds of letters as well. In addition, she brought up her children, became entangled in passionate love affairs, travelled across Europe when travel was not easy even in times of peace, entertained her numerous friends lavishly and conversed with them as readily as she drew breath.

Where did she find the time to think about her work? This question occupied her contemporaries. According to her cousin and intimate friend, Mme Albertine Necker de Saussure, author of a most sensitive study of Mme de Staël's character and writings, the creator of *Corinne* allotted no special time for thought. On one occasion, remarking that Germaine had slept all night and had been busy or engaged in talk all day, Mme Necker de Saussure inquired when the plan for her latest work had been laid out. Mme de Staël laughed and answered: 'In my sedan chair'. Germaine was only in her sedan chair very briefly, yet the subject for each chapter was already decided, observed her cousin, who drew the conclusion that there must have been very few moments when Mme de Staël was not thinking and working. It was Germaine's custom to carry from room to room a small writing-case of green morocco leather that contained her work and correspondence. This she would keep ready on her knees wherever she was, even surrounded by people. No little tension was betrayed by her frequent habit of twisting a small piece of greenery, prepared for her by a servant.

How did she manage to do so much? Clearly, she must have been a person of immense energies and determination as well as talent. She admired energy in others, and despised sloth and indifference. Of course, she was sustained by great wealth, and by being able to call upon the assistance of an army of servants. There are often allusions to members of her staff in her autobiographical writings or letters. These included personal maids, governesses, companions, as well as business agents and trusted confidential menservants who might be charged with the task of bringing some recalcitrant lover to heel. Then there were the scholars and cultivated friends who formed her circle, and who from time to time pursued researches on her behalf. As 'Necker's daughter', too, she inherited a network of relationships among the crowned heads, the nobility, the political leaders and men of letters (a network that she herself vastly enlarged). In this system of support from servants, savants and world-wide connections, upon whom she could call from her beginnings as an artist, she differed from most of her less prosperous and less fortunate successors among creative women writers.

What was the link between the manifold spheres of her writing, her activities and her life? It was freedom. She wanted freedom for everyone as well as herself: freedom for thought and self-expression; freedom for growth in individuals and peoples, who must be allowed to live independently in accordance with their own inner being or character. Living to the full was what mattered, but in her view there could be no genuine life without freedom to change and develop. There might be disadvantages, but then, as she often allowed, everything in human affairs had disadvantages. These one must strive to overcome.

For the purposes of discussion, it will be necessary to separate the various branches of her ideas, her action and her art. Yet, in a certain sense, this separation is artificial. For few of her works are confined to a single area or theme. *Corinne, or Italy* reveals in its title that it is more than a novel, and that it concerns the destiny of a nation as well as that of its heroine. Mme de Staël's penetrating book, *On the Influence of the Passions*, only partly completed, deals with politics and political passions as well as with her own personal disillusionment. Her volume *On Literature* treats of more than literature: it embraces the whole area of past and present intellectual endeavour known to her. As for *On Germany*, it is not only about that country but about her own reflections on life, political action, art, womanhood; it is also a weapon in her battle to defeat materialist philosophy. The study entitled *Considerations on the Principal Events of the French Revolution* deals only in part with the history of that cataclysm: within this extraordinary work there can be found also an account of Necker's stewardship, a comparison between it and Napoleon's, to the latter's detriment, together with proposals for the way the country should be rightly governed.

For each of her books she prepared a formal plan. Under major headings there were numerous subdivisions. The whole assumed the shape of a reasoned argument: sometimes she would reply to hypothetical objections to her views. Yet beneath this often deceptive neo-classical formality, there runs a subterranean passion that frequently breaks the banks of the form. New and often brilliant ideas are cast up and scattered here and there, to be developed by later poets, dramatists and critics. To pursue these ideas the reader escapes along varied paths that at first do not always seem to connect with the coolly proposed formal argument. Sometimes, the writing can resemble a fascinating conversation, with its twists and turns in all directions, its dazzling insights, rather than carefully worked literary prose. That is not to deny the moments of great and vivid eloquence, of impassioned indignation or prophetic vision. But it helps to explain the verbosity that Stendhal complained about, the looseness of expression noticed by Maria Edgeworth, which must be partly due to Mme de Staël's manner of working amid so many distractions. The amazing thing is that, given those surrounding diversions, she was able to think and write to such purpose.

Fame was the spur. To equal somehow the hour of triumph of Necker's recall in 1789: that was the secret ambition. It appeared in the potent fantasy of the poet Corinne's coronation at the Capitol in Rome. The streets were decorated; everywhere one heard talk of Corinne's manifold talents. Rich, independent, nobly-born, Corinne is seen as 'a goddess surrounded by clouds'. Her chariot, built in antique style, is drawn by four white horses; young girls clothed in white walk beside her. She is dressed like the Sibyl in Domenichino's painting, with an exotic Indian silk head-dress that resembles the turbans favoured by her creator. Corinne may be brilliant, but she is also womanly: 'Her pose on the chariot was noble and modest: one could tell that she was pleased to be admired; but a feeling of timidity mingled with her joy, and seemed to ask forgiveness for her triumph; . . . she gave at once the impression of a priestess of Apollo moving towards the Temple of the Sun, and of a perfectly simple woman pursuing the ordinary course of life . . .'. Corinne has everything, in short. Her triumph, when she is acclaimed by the Roman people and by her peers, is set in the winter of 1794/5. The novel was published in 1807, when Germaine was already famous, but before she was to achieve the immense celebrity of her last years — a celebrity that would far outshine her father's.

That great fame, which Germaine had so desired, carried drawbacks for the author as much as for her heroine. Was it truly deserved, and how far has it survived? That is what will now be considered in her different fields of endeavour.

Literature

When Mme de Staël thought of literature, she did not envisage it as something limited to essays, poetry, fiction, drama. She extolled 'the importance of literature, considered in its widest sense, that is, including philosophical writings as well as works of imagination, indeed, everything that concerns the exercise of thought in writing, except physical sciences'. Thus, under the heading of literature, she embraced not only poetry and eloquence but history and philosophy (or, as she called it, the study of man's moral or inner life). Imagination and thought: these were the twin aspects of literature she probed and united in her own work. Literature assumed a great importance for her because she was writing at a time when the written word was acquiring more power and influence through the rise of the press, and the growing prominence of the novel as a genre. Besides, she could perceive that literature, in the wide sense she gave the term, was inseparable from human freedom, which it needed to breathe, flourish and survive. At the same time, she was among the first to see that literature had a vital part to play in the enduring cause of freedom itself. Essentially, it was not licence that she advocated, but freedom with order.

Her novels offer one aspect of her work that has not worn particularly well. One reason for this is her debt to the novelistic conventions of the day: for example, the presentation of Delphine as little short of an angel, notwithstanding that heroine's imprudence (always the result of generous motives). To prove Oswald's right to be the hero of *Corinne*, he has nobly to save the city of Ancona from destruction by fire virtually single-handed, contriving to rescue first the Jews from the ghetto and then the insane from the asylum, in the face of superstition, antagonism or indifference. Yet in other respects, Mme de Staël shows Oswald to be weak and vacillating. Indeed, it is the pull between the contemporary claims of the 'sublime' in art and the depiction of ordinary feelings (which, as she proved in her *Essay on Fiction*, she wanted in the modern novel) that provides much of the interest of her fiction today. Her novels betray the tension between her ideal self-image and her real self-knowledge.

Besides these concessions of hers to certain popular expectations in the novel of her day, there was her lack of invention in the creation of a convincing plot. The far-fetched dénouement and the two separate conclusions to *Delphine* bear witness to this deficiency. Quite early she was perfectly aware of this failing, for she told Fanny Burney's sister, Mrs Phillips, that the 'power of forming a new ingenious yet *natural* Story was what she felt most deficient in '. True, this remark of hers was made before she had written her two novels, but she had already composed several stories. The want of conviction, force and control in the narrative as a whole is, however, counterbalanced by her gift of psychological penetration. There is considerable skill in the way the reader of *Delphine* is led to sense the hand of Mme de Vernon behind all Léonce's misconceptions about the woman he loves.

Mme de Staël's novels are concerned with the sufferings of woman in a cold, frivolous egotistical society — even Mme de Vernon's ruse and dissimulation are rooted in her cruel upbringing and forced marriage. These novels also portray what a contemporary critic in the *Edinburgh Review* called 'the heartlessness of polished men'. The professed lover (Léonce or Oswald) who should sustain and protect the heroine, lamentably fails her. Stendhal once went so far as to say that Léonce does not really love Delphine — and certainly that paragon of honour always seems ready to sacrifice her to his code. Oswald, too, sacrifices Corinne to his wish for an orderly, conventional life, and forfeits her esteem. These rare women of refined and passionate sensibility are, in short, doomed to separation and loss.

How far did Mme de Staël accept the canons of the society

against which she rebelled in her novels (and, indeed, even more thunderously, in her own style of life)? Certainly, her mockery of the trivial chat of the English ladies at the tea-table in *Corinne* is amusing, and one can readily imagine how the great Parisian conversationalist must have suffered at similar insipid entertainments offered to her by English hostesses. Yet despite her satire of a tedious common round, or her sharp portrayal of the shallowness and hypocrisy of Parisian high life in *Delphine*, at times in her novels she yields to current social forces, by making concessions to accepted criteria on such matters as feminine weakness and the virtues of domesticity and submission. Nothing reveals so well the power of fashionable society and its codes in her day, or the extent of the courage that was needed to defy them in any particular. This element of defiance is what appealed to French writers who came after her, and who were to stress the revolt of superior, misunderstood individuals against a repressive society.

Readers in Mme de Staël's day tended to be far more patient than their modern counterparts. Her contemporaries were usually quite readily inclined to follow the protagonist's vicissitudes, together with reflections on important matters of morality and religion, at great length through several volumes. If Mme de Staël did not offer them a strong narrative line, instead she offered them something else: a new way of examining a society and of probing the social standards and attitudes that moulded and deformed people's lives. She exposed the very different possibilities open to men and women, and she implied some hope of a change in consciousness and manners, if readers drew the right conclusion.

Where *Delphine* is concerned with contemporary French society and the problems it raised, *Corinne* occupies the broader canvas of northern and southern Europe, and must have provided a painless form of education as well as a story. Jane Austen might choose to recommend *Corinne* to a gentleman who was stone deaf, presumably thereby hinting ironically at the book's operatic character; but here was no small piece of ivory to be intricately worked to perfection; here was a slab of marble to be hewn at no little risk into a monument. One can readily imagine what a breath of fresh air *Corinne* must have brought to many people who were isolated and confined within a narrow circle in some small town or village, and who had little chance of escape. In imagination, they could linger in the Campagna; they, too, could be moved by the ruins of the Roman forum; reflect on past and present; observe picturesque customs; consort with modern Italian writers, musicians and artists, and discover the latest theories on the arts; think about nationhood; learn without strain how to look at their world in a fresh, life-giving way.

Corinne is a novel of a distinct kind — what Sainte-Beuve was to call a 'novel-poem', by which he doubtless meant that it did not rely on narrative alone but on the creation of a poetic vision. It was to have numerous imitators in the nineteenth century who were not primarily concerned with 'realism' but with the projection of some form of inner crisis or spiritual enlightenment. As a novel, *Corinne* seems more modern in its disregard of 'realistic' form than *Delphine* with its reliance on letters. Both, however, are landmarks in the history of fiction: *Delphine* stands as a forerunner of the social novel that alludes to urgent social issues and intends some ultimate transformation; while *Corinne* remains one of the greatest myth-making books of all time.

With *Corinne*, Mme de Staël invented the richly creative myth of the independent woman of genius, about whom more will have to be said. She also propagated there the myth of the artist ineluctably doomed to suffering. Moreover, she helped to popularize the dream of Italy as the desired land of beauty and art that has endured to our own day. No longer was Italy the preserve of writers and artists, or of aristocrats on the Grand Tour: through *Corinne* it had become transformed into the essential spiritual patrimony of all those who aspired to culture and civilization.

As a literary critic, too, Mme de Staël made a large contribution. She took from eighteenth-century works, which she had studied in her youth, certain hints whose potential had not been fully realized, or certain productive notions that had not been applied to literature. These she welded together into a coherent shape, a logical whole, which in turn presented entirely new possibilities for the reader to pursue.

It has been said that Mme de Staël invented the study known as comparative literature. To compare was her forte: she understood what stimulating discoveries could be made by comparing one literature with another, for instance, the writings of northern and southern Europe as exemplified for her in Ossian and

Homer. In a note to her book *On Literature*, she indicated how well she realized the novelty of her approach in discussing the distinction between French wit and English humour.

Besides, she believed that there was nothing but benefit to be gained from the contact between literatures, expounding in *On Germany* the work of German poets, dramatists and philosophers in order to stimulate her inward-looking French readers and colleagues, whom she found to be excessively complacent in their belief in the superiority of their own taste. At first, many were outraged at this insult to French pre-eminence. However, others soon understood how valuable *On Germany* could be to them, and proceeded to plunder the book in their quest for fresh images and themes. She did much the same for the Italians. Among Mme de Staël's last works was an essay entitled *On the Spirit of Translations*, first published amid great controversy in Italy in 1816, where she advised the Italians to profit from new productions in English and German in order to create a truly modern Italian literature.

Moreover, it was Mme de Staël who, with others, helped to create literary and artistic history (according to the liberal historian, Benedetto Croce). It was she who, in *On Germany*, divided literature into periods of the human spirit:

> It seems as if the philosophical march of the human spirit should be divided into four different ages: heroic times which established civilization; patriotism, which shaped antiquity's glory; chivalry, the warrior religion of Europe; and the love of liberty, whose history began around the epoch of the Reformation.

This division of literary studies into distinct periods, even though the choice of the various categories might be very different from hers, has become so much a part of the way literature has been studied that it is taken for granted.

Another notion that has been totally absorbed into the modern study of literature is her belief that literary works cannot be separated from the government and institutions, the society and the history of a country, nor should they be examined in isolation from the other arts, such as painting and music. This is made clear throughout *Corinne* as well as *On Germany*. Mme de Staël was moved less by painting than by music, and so she took advice on the fine arts, where her taste inclined to neo-classical narrative pictures. She tended to prefer Italian music to German. Her appreciation of Haydn and Mozart, whose works she heard in Vienna, may seem rather reserved today, but what really counts is that she was trying to achieve the seemingly impossible, to embrace all manifestations of a culture. One might say of such an ambition, however far it fell short of its aim, that it was not mean, and that it set a standard and stretched the imagination.

It was Mme de Staël who drew the conclusion that, since literature was inseparable from governments, from social and political institutions that determined its nature, it must necessarily be quite different under a republic from what it had been under an absolute monarchy. After the Revolution had occurred, it was no use trying to insist on keeping 'rules' which had been formulated to suit the taste of a monarchical society. The French Revolution she conceived not as an accident but as an event of colossal importance, the beginning of a new era for the life of the mind. It was essential now to avoid all those theories that stifle talent, and to adopt new standards of judgement to fit a changed world. Instead of submitting to the reign of accepted 'good taste', writers must henceforward rely on their own personal impressions, 'on what one has felt oneself', as she remarked significantly in *On Literature*. One can imagine how such views served to liberate writers from the restrictions under which they had laboured, how henceforward they would have the dizzy freedom — and the heavy responsibility — to be true to their own inner being.

In this manner Mme de Staël did much to bring about an entirely new spirit in literature. She helped to educate her readers to look for something authentic — true both to themselves and to the national culture. It was she who introduced to the French public the word 'Romantic' as applied to poetry, having first heard of it in Germany. For her, Romantic poetry is primarily governed by inspiration, not imitation. Romantic literature 'is indigenous to us', she assured her contemporaries, 'and it is our religion and our institutions that have made it flower'. And because such literature has its roots in our own soil, she added, 'it is the only one that can grow and be revivified . . .'. With her, the concept of the 'Romantic' is accompanied by the idea of modernity: 'Nothing in art must be stationary', she wrote, 'and art

becomes petrified when it ceases to change'. Consequently, literature has its own literary revolution to balance political revolution.
The new will become the desirable norm. Mme de Staël perceived within herself and her contemporaries a new kind of
sensibility, born 'in modern times', defining it as 'this restless
reflection which often devours us like the vulture of Prometheus'.
She helped to foster this modern self-conscious sensibility
through her writings, and in this she proved a significant pioneer.
Indeed, she issued what was later regarded as the first Romantic
manifesto in France.

Much as she admired 'art', artistic perfection does not seem to
have been her chief consideration as a writer: that was liberty.
Having seen how literature had changed its nature in the eighteenth century, how it had become 'a weapon for the human
spirit', she herself wielded words as weapons in the struggle for
justice and humane values against the dark forces of fanaticism
and authoritarianism. Mme de Staël was thus a consciously
'committed' writer, for whom writing was primarily a form of
action.

Thought and Action

Few grasped better than the author of *On Literature* the modern
temptations connected with political action. She observed how
her contemporaries were engaging in political activity in order to
cover the sense of disillusion, the feeling of 'emptiness' and
'nothingness' (such as she herself constantly experienced), the
awareness of 'the incompleteness of destiny', as she called it. 'The
terrible events we have witnessed have dulled the sensibility', she
wrote, referring to the Terror, 'and everything that relates to
thought seems lack-lustre beside the omnipotence of action'.

Speaking of the young men who were influenced by the violent
deeds of the outlaw, Karl Moor, in Schiller's play, *The Brigands*,
she noted perspicaciously: 'They thought they felt indignant
about abuses in the social order, when they were merely weary of
their own personal situation'. She had noticed, too, how during
the Revolution, one of the great attractions for people hitherto
totally occupied with the monotonous task of earning a livelihood, was 'the very agitation' which it brought into their tedious

lives: 'The swift succession of events, the emotions this aroused, caused a kind of intoxication which made time move faster, and no longer allowed the void or the disquiet of existence to be felt'. Such action principally to cover private emptiness, met with her disapproval since it is founded on a negative element. She could analyse this type of activity so well because she had been tempted to it herself.

Elsewhere in her writings, action is seen as necessary and valuable, but it is action in a rather different sense. Action as the expression of 'energy', even though it may result in crimes which she would otherwise abhor, is considered necessary for progress.

> Although strong passions lead to crimes which indifference would never have caused, there are circumstances in history where these passions are necessary to rewind the clock of society . . . . Violent upheavals are necessary to bring the human spirit to entirely new purposes: they are earthquakes, subterranean forces, which reveal to man's gaze buried riches; time alone would not have sufficed to excavate a path to these.

This exculpation of violence in terms of necessity forms part of her apology for the French Revolution, and of revolution in general. It contradicts the loathing of violence she often expressed so forcibly.

German writers in particular are reproved for being excessively concerned with thought at the expense of action. Speculative thinkers in Germany 'yield willingly enough to the powers-that-be everything that is real in life'. They are daring in their thought but submissively obedient to authority in their conduct. Consequently, they lack 'the energy of action' to be found in free countries (Mme de Staël had her favourite model, England, in mind). Here, action is seen as eminently desirable when it has the positive aim of patriotic resistance to injustice and oppression. Mme de Staël was writing these words before the rise of a concerted national movement in Germany to resist Napoleon. Goethe would say of *On Germany* in 1814 that, had the book appeared sooner, people would have attributed to it an influence on recent important occurrences, but that now it seemed like a prophecy after the event.

Germaine de Staël's encouragement of positive action can be

found also in her discussion of the dramatist Alfieri in *Corinne*: 'He was born for action', she declared, 'yet he could do nothing but write . . .'. Alfieri's frustration in this regard was, in her opinion, entirely due to the decadent state of Italy in his day. 'He wished to attain a political aim through literature: this aim was doubtless the noblest of all.' She added, however, that nothing so distorts works of the imagination as to have such an aim. From this, it seems clear that Mme de Staël, while advocating an active role for writers in the pursuit of freedom and justice, did not favour those who in drama — or in poetry and novels — deliberately set out to foster a cause. A political aim should only be pursued obliquely in creative works: this was the method she herself tried to employ, though often the thesis becomes too evident in her own novels.

When her friends advised her to be more circumspect in discussing controversial matters, Mme de Staël used to reply: 'It is the truth, it is what I think and I shall say so'. Certainly, she spoke and wrote the truth as she saw it with admirable courage and disregard for the consequences. Yet she could flatter, as Byron observed. There were areas, too, where she was inclined to fudge the strict truth. She ignored German Francophobia, for instance, in *On Germany*, presumably because it would have interfered with her effort to show German culture as eminently worthy.

In her writings on politics, she was apt to conceal the extent of her own role and activity. It is not easy to tell exactly the degree of her involvement in the *coup d'état* of 18 Fructidor 1797, or in General Moreau's conspiracy of 1802. In her account of the persecution she suffered under Napoleon, she liked to portray herself as a timid female without protection or support, a passive victim. This she certainly was not. No 'feeble' woman would have fostered the careers of Narbonne, Talleyrand and Constant; would have ventured into Russia at the time of the Napoleonic invasion; would have worked so ardently for the emperor's downfall by promoting the cause of Bernadotte.

Doubtless she felt that to reveal the details of such political activity would be detrimental to her feminine image, already challenged by virulently hostile critics. Given the attitudes of the day towards woman's role in society, including the commonly proposed view that women, like children, should be seen and not heard, such a concession to established manners seems readily understandable. Equally comprehensible is her declared (and genuine) respect for the code of morality — more honoured in the breach than in the observance by her contemporaries — however much her own conduct as an independent woman who took a succession of ill-chosen lovers might deviate from it.

Passion was what counted for her. It was a token of energy. It stood above the laws, proclaimed the betrayed eponymous heroine of her early story, *Zulma*. Yet even when in the power of her emotions, Germaine de Staël could be capable of self-analysis. She knew when she was moving out of control even though she felt she could do nothing to prevent it. In her study of the passions, she discussed this condition:

A kind of philosophy in the mind, independent of the very nature of one's character, allows one to judge oneself as an outsider, without knowledge influencing decision; to watch oneself suffer, without one's pain being alleviated by the gift of self-observation.

Corinne, who rashly travels in despair to Scotland to catch a glimpse of the elusive Oswald, speaks of 'my sad gift of observing my own folly'. Both Delphine and Corinne have moments when they feel themselves to be outsiders, as they hover unseen at some glittering social ceremony — a marriage or a ball — that seals their private unhappiness. In *On Literature*, Mme de Staël spoke of 'reflective passion that judges and knows itself without being able to control itself'. According to her, both Rousseau and Goethe had preceded her in the depiction of 'reflective passion'. It was she who defined it.

Mme de Staël inherited the aristocratic notion of a hierarchy of souls after Rousseau had injected into it the quality of passionate sensibility. As her cousin relates, the author of *On the Influence of the Passions* divided people into two classes: sensitive souls (including herself) and frigid, mediocre souls. By 1800, Mme de Staël saw mediocrity as all-powerful. Exceptional creatures were being obliged to dim their light because of the pervasive influence of the mediocre. Society itself, she would write later, was governed by coldness and egotism. Her book on the passions dealt solely with passionate sensitive spirits, she insisted; it was directed to them; it did not concern those who had never been governed by passion.

Passion spelt suffering, by definition. Individuals and nations might set out in quest of happiness (her own goal and that of France at the Revolution), but it was doomed to failure. As she wrote in her study of the passions, 'Happiness, as man conceives it, is absolutely impossible'. And she added: 'The man who would devote himself to perfect felicity would be the most unfortunate of beings; the nation that would seek to attain to the abstract limit of metaphysical freedom would be the most wretched . . .'. This double insight into the limitations of human happiness in both the private and the political realm was due to her disillusion with Narbonne, and with the way the Revolution had been sullied by violence and cruelty when men proposed to establish unadulterated happiness and freedom on earth.

Mme de Staël was speaking of her own youthful illusions when she wrote of the 'trust with which you forge ahead into life'. In youth, all you have heard of human wickedness you regard as belonging to history, she declared; you do not think it can affect yourself. But then you are made to realize that trusted friends can prove unworthy: 'In the end, the heart withers, life grows colourless, you in your turn behave badly, so that you are as disgusted with yourself as with others.' Suicide then appeared as a real temptation that long haunted her.

From about 1793, this sense of disillusion underlies all her writings. Yet she refused to yield to it. She preserved, as it were against the odds, an awareness that the living must be on the side of life. So, after Condorcet, she could advance the theory of 'indefinite perfectibility' in *On Literature*, the idea of a constant progress in the history of the human spirit, notwithstanding all the savagery that runs counter to it. This progress, she declared, could be found principally in philosophy and science, not in imaginative literature and the fine arts.

For her, the movement of progress was mysterious. There were times when humanity moved back, and times when it moved forward a little, for example in the greater number of those admitted to the status of human beings (whether classes, slaves, or women). 'Each time some inferior class has emerged from slavery or degradation, humankind has grown . . .more perfect', she maintained. This did not mean that total perfection would ever be attained under any system in some remote future. By 1800 she had made the discovery that the progress of science should ideally be accompanied by moral progress: 'for, in increasing man's power, one must strengthen the restraint which prevents him from abusing it'. Her view of 'indefinite perfectibility', much misunderstood, was grounded in a sense of human error and backsliding.

How could such human error be counterbalanced? There should be a mathematical method of examining facts and counting instances that would enable administrators to deal properly with various recurring problems. She observed that in the Canton of Berne the number of divorces was being studied every ten years, while the number of murders was being recorded each year in some Italian towns. 'This is what should incline one to think that political science can one day acquire the clarity of geometry', she wrote hopefully in *On the Influence of the Passions*, published in 1796. Four years later she was still concerned, after Condorcet, with the question of using statistics to make political calculations. By such means, she thought, one might even be able to know the opinion of an assembly beforehand. Mme de Staël, like the *idéologues*, sought for a form of political science based on solid principles. Here again, she was a pioneer.

In other respects, however, in psychology and philosophy, Mme de Staël did not favour *idéologues* like Destutt de Tracy with their materialist theories. Instead, she fought against the utilitarianism of Helvétius and Bentham, her book *On Germany* being the culmination of that struggle. It was her view that a morality based on self-interest leads directly to the yoke of authoritarianism. As she said succinctly in a footnote on Bentham: 'Utility is necessarily modified by circumstances: virtue should never be.' That is why she lauded 'enthusiasm', an awareness of the divine, that inspired zeal which she translated as 'God in us'. Without such an awareness, she felt, there could be no sustaining hope of a reunion with her father in an afterlife; without it, there could be no response to beauty, no magnanimity, no self-sacrifice.

Politics and Morality

Inheriting from her father the belief that morality should be the essential guide in politics, Mme de Staël could write in her analysis of the passions: 'I think that true morality . . . is in harmony with the general interest'. In an age pervaded by cynicism, by the desire for private advantage, by the notion of the so-called 'supreme law' of the good of 'the People', she tried to uphold the values of the Christian ethic. Yet this was modified somewhat by the aristocratic code with its conviction that greatness of soul could be found in great crime as well as in great virtue.

Although Mme de Staël felt that the French Revolution had taken the wrong path under Robespierre and the Terror, she never repudiated the Revolution itself. She belonged with those who thought it had been betrayed. The cruelty and barbarism that had stained the Revolution were the consequence of centuries of oppression, poverty, superstition and ignorance. It was ill-treatment that led to mob violence. Still, the faults caused by passion were often the sign of some higher faculty. Certainly, where the criminal acts of great men were concerned, 'powerful and generous qualities make one overlook criminal excesses, provided that the mark of greatness is imprinted on the brow of the offender'. In her early writings, she did not appear inclined to attribute such crimes to human evil.

By the time Mme de Staël came to write *On Germany*, though, she acknowledged that evil could not be denied: 'Whatever the good intentions of the partisans of optimism, more profundity can be observed, it seems to me, in those who do not deny evil, but who understand the relationship between this evil and man's freedom'. All the same, there are far less allusions in her work to an explanation of political crime in terms of individual evil, than in terms of the oppressive acts of societies and regimes. This attitude of hers is characteristic of the liberal outlook, and one token of its limitations.

The Reign of Terror altered her youthful view that, with the Revolution, humanity was set on an upward path. She spent much time brooding on the Terror and trying to explain it to her own satisfaction. She wanted to convince herself that the tyranny of Robespierre and the crimes of the *enragés* could not be renewed:

. . .this era is outside the course of nature, beyond crime; and, for the sake of public tranquillity, we must convince ourselves that, since no plan can lead us to foresee or explain such atrocities, this chance conjunction of every kind of moral monstrosity is an exceptional accident that thousands of centuries cannot repeat.

These words seem to be an expression of hope rather than of firm belief, a hope that would be tragically doomed to disappointment.

What distinguished the Terror in Mme de Staël's eyes from earlier examples of butchery was its cold deliberation. Acts of cruelty committed in the heat of the moment could not be compared

with what we have seen in our day, an uninterrupted and hence emotionless method, aimed at the disregard of compassion . . . . Woe, then, to the leaders who, stifling everything humane in their supporters, turn them into reasoning murderers, who advance into crime by way of metaphysics . . .!

Here, Mme de Staël was pointing to murders carried out in the name of a political system or ideology. In the case of the Terror, with its assumption of guilt by association, the aim was the annihilation of a class, the aristocracy, in order to institute the reign of 'virtue'. She saw that here was the birth of ideological murder.

Political fanaticism had no greater opponent than Mme de Staël, who realized that in modern times it had taken the place of religious fanaticism. What she had to say about both political and religious fanaticism still carries weight today, when these twin scourges once again proliferate. As a disciple of the Enlightenment, she attacked such excessive zeal in her early political writings and throughout her work with great force and eloquence. During the French Revolution, she observed, opposing factions were equally absolute in their opinions, used the same kind of extreme language, and behaved with equal lack of tolerance. Once the members of a faction were in the grip of blind political passion, their reason and feeling were silenced. Such men were then spared the hard effort of comparing, balancing, modifying their arguments. The cause itself was transformed into a savage god, in whose service there could be no remorse. These members of a faction mingled solely with people who shared their own opinions. Any opponent ceased to appear to them as a human being and became expendable.

This clear-sighted analysis of bigotry did not prevent her from working ardently for moderation and reconciliation. On the contrary, it made her more determined in her quest for the middle path. Yet she knew only too well, from her father's experience as well as her own, how such political fanatics hated the moderates perhaps even more than they hated anyone. Her central position between bitterly opposing factions highlights the liberal dilemma. The extreme position all too often proves more attractive to weaker spirits than the middle way. The moderates may well find themselves crushed between opposing extremes. Mme de Staël herself came under their double fire, but she was quite capable of returning it.

She loathed violence as much as she hated fanaticism, and she was fond of quoting Jean-Jacques Rousseau, who said 'that it was not permissible for a nation to purchase the most desirable Revolution with the blood of a single innocent'. According to her, 'these simple words contain all that is true, sacred, divine in human destiny'.

Mme de Staël exposed the new tendency to drown compassion by an appeal not just to the present fate of the nation as a whole, but also to the destiny of humanity in the future. Current ills were being depicted 'as the means, as the guarantee of an immortal future, a political happiness above all the sacrifices demanded to obtain it', she wrote, adding:

> If we were convinced of one single principle, that men have not the right to do evil to attain to good, we would not have seen so many human victims slain on the very altar of the virtues. But since these dealings have existed between the present and the future, between the sacrifice of the present generation and the gifts to be made to the generation of the future, there have been no limits that some fresh intensity of passion might not arrogate to itself the right to cross . . . .

These words were written when the Terror was vividly in her mind.

A few years later Mme de Staël complained that during the Terror many decent people accepted employment in the administration, and even on the revolutionary tribunals, 'either to do good or to diminish evil that was being committed. All based themselves on a fairly common type of reasoning: that they prevented a scoundrel from occupying the post and thus helped the oppressed. To employ evil means for an end one believes to be good is an extremely bad principle'. This was because of the limitations of human nature: 'Men know nothing of the future, nothing of themselves for tomorrow. . . ' On the notion that the end justifies the means, Mme de Staël was adamant: it was a source of error and evil. Whether the end was the salvation of humankind in 'the future', or the 'public safety' in the present, she condemned it unequivocally.

When, at the bloodiest period of the Revolution, they wanted to sanction every crime, they called the government 'the Committee of Public Safety'; thereby proclaiming the well-known maxim, that the welfare of the people is the supreme law. The supreme law is justice.

Mme de Staël analysed with great clarity dangerous underlying trends in the French Revolution, trends that would become ever more influential, and would endure down to our own day.

It seemed to her at first that the Terror was, for those who lived through it, something for which there was no existing language. 'No, even to-day, reasoning cannot approach this period which stands beyond the common measure. To judge these events . . . is to put them back into the order of existing ideas, ideas for which there already was a terminology.' This sense of an atrocity so extreme as to be beyond the sphere of the known and the expressible is one that has recurred since. Yet she struggled to find words to try to cope with it.

The language of politics, and its debasement in the Revolution, concerned her deeply. She criticized the inflated and arid style of revolutionary invective, which could be literally fatal for the person under attack, offering as an example: 'Cato is a counter-revolutionary in the pay of our enemies, and I demand the death of this great criminal in order to appease national justice.' She stigmatized also the proliferation of revolutionary jargon. The truth was lost under its monotonous, soul-destroying litany of exaggerated and empty set phrases.

In her *Considerations on the Principal Events of the French Revolution*, Mme de Staël published the first great book of the nineteenth century to examine what happened during the upheaval and after, the tendencies that surfaced, and their significance. In that book, she tried to show what attitudes, what values, methods, institutions and guarantees were needed to establish the freedom of the individual under the protection of the laws. It was far safer to take as one's guiding thread the welfare of the individual than some high-sounding and unrealizable ideal, theory or system. The supreme value of the individual and of individual freedom would remain the corner-stone of the liberal edifice. The problem for her was how to avoid the domination of one class or one man.

When Mme de Staël began writing about politics, the word 'libéral' used in French in a political sense was fairly recent, and it only became current in that sense when she was in her early thirties. She spoke of the 'liberal idea' in her study of the passions; of the 'liberal impetus' in her book *On Germany*; of 'liberal principles' and 'a purely liberal and peaceful policy' in her *Considerations*. Indeed, as the disciple of Montesquieu, she was one of the principal founders of nineteenth-century liberalism in France. It was to her writings, and especially to her *Considerations*, that later French liberals looked for guidance. At the same time, opponents of liberalism found there a coherent body of views to attack. As Mme Necker de Saussure said of the *Considerations*: 'It was the first time that the apology of liberal ideas made an impression on those whose interest it was to repel them'. Mme de Staël not only stated the essential principles of French liberalism, she also gave expression to a number of problems that oppress the liberal spirit.

What is Mme de Staël's concept of liberty? It is rooted in obedience to law. It is 'the feeling of justice, the dignity of all classes, firmness of principles, respect for enlightenment and for individual merit', she declared in *Considerations*. In her view, the remedy for mob violence lies 'not in despotism but in the rule of law'. Speaking of the revolutionary clubs that functioned outside the Assembly during the Revolution, she observed:

As soon as we permit within a government a power which is not legal, it always ends by becoming the stronger. As it has no other functions except to blame what is done, and not to act itself, it escapes criticism, and its supporters include all those who desire change in the state . . . . The Jacobin clubs were organized like a government, more so than the government itself: . . . they should have been regarded as the subterranean mine always ready to explode existing institutions, when the opportunity should arise.

Civil liberties for all were vital. 'The chief foundation of all liberty is individual guarantees . . .', she remarked in *Considerations*. Writing to Benjamin Constant when he was preparing the Additional Act, Napoleon's liberal constitution, in 1815, she urged: 'If it is true that you are working on the constitution, I advise you to think more about guarantees than about declarations of rights'. It is no wonder that she recommended great care in protecting the interests of the accused, or that she regarded appeal courts and a free press as guarantees against injustice. She was not likely ever to forget that her father had been banished by *lettre de cachet* (the King's command given under the royal seal); and that she herself had been sent into exile by Napoleon without any form of trial or possibility of appeal.

Mme de Staël did not favour the word 'democracy' (which had not yet become included among the virtues). Writing in the early 1790s, she observed in a note: 'The word "democracy" being taken to-day in several senses, it would not precisely render what I wish to express'. (Indeed, the Revolution would see the birth of what has been called totalitarian democracy, as well as that of the liberal variety.) She wanted a form of government by an élite whose aim was 'the happiness of all'. There must be equality before the law, but not an 'abstract equality' elevated into a system. Far more important to her than the false goal of abstract equality was what she called competition and the equality of opportunity that would enable merit to rise.

Essential to her political views, as we have seen when they were expressed under the Directory, was the notion of the importance of property and its value as a stabilizing element. Yet, through her trust in the gradual enlightenment of the majority, she expected people to acquire property through their own enterprise, and hence to attain both a sense of responsibility and the necessary condition which would enable them to participate through elections in the affairs of the nation. Given the appalling and uneducated state of the underprivileged in her day — and having witnessed how they could be misled and their dangerous passions aroused by demagogues, or how they adored her *bête noire*, the tyrant Napoleon, who did nothing for them — she was perhaps not entirely unreasonable in thinking that they were not yet ready for power. She did, however, want everyone to be treated with fairness. Those she referred to as 'the lower classes' of society must not be left in physical want — but she did not say how this improvement was to be achieved, except by means of greater enlightenment.

Although she proved to be quite skilful in managing her own financial affairs after Necker's death, she was not really very interested in the administration of the material resources of the country. Her concern was the achievement of 'proven ideas in political science', as she put it in her book on the passions. At a time when Robespierre and Saint-Just were forced to consider (in theory at least) a new distribution of wealth to the poor and hungry, and were promulgating decrees that led to an economic dictatorship; at a time when 'Gracchus' Babeuf was conspiring to establish political communism in France, Mme de Staël was functioning on a completely different level. The great failing of her liberal thought, despite her honest concern to improve the condition of 'the lower classes', was the omission of necessary measures to be taken to that end, measures to alleviate poverty and starvation that should have been as vital as the cause of civil liberty. Instead, this function was to be left ever more in the hands of those who were indifferent or hostile to individual freedom, and who did all they could to discredit it.

The political liberals who would form the opposition under the Bourbon Restoration of Louis XVIII and his brother Charles X, and who would attain power after the July Revolution of 1830 and the advent of the House of Orléans with Louis-Philippe, looked back to Mme de Staël and the *Considerations*. Yet their triumph under the Orléanist regime — characterized for many of its critics by the domination of a single class, the higher bourgeoisie; by Guizot's notorious advice to 'Get rich!'; and by vulgar mediocrity and corruption — would scarcely have appealed to the author of *Corinne*, the advocate of 'enthusiasm', had she lived to see it. The cause of political liberalism, as she envisaged it, was not fated ultimately to prosper in France.

As for the liberal Bonapartists, who derived largely from Napoleon's liberal phase of 1815, Mme de Staël had urged liberals to separate their own cause from the emperor's, and to take care 'not to confuse the principles of the Revolution with those of the imperial regime'. She had noted only too well the abasement of certain libertarians before Napoleon's dazzling power. On no account, she insisted, should Bonapartists be included among those who upheld the principles of liberty in France. The trouble was that Bonaparte himself had always contrived to appear to many as the heir of the French Revolution of 1789, and none of Mme de Staël's warnings about the despot succeeded in removing the equivocation from which his heirs would profit.

Still, during the First Empire and the Bourbon Restoration, Mme de Staël did embody the hopes of a great many people in Europe who understood her true meaning. In Italy, for instance, the writer Silvio Pellico (who was to be kept in prison for nine years) said that the *Considerations* would do a great deal of good in Europe, and that true liberals could only profit from the work. Pellico thought that no other book had revealed in so masterly a way the character of the lofty tyrant and the infamous nature of his system of government.

What Mme de Staël understood quite early was that Bonaparte was restoring a form of monarchy even more absolute in some respects than that which had been swept away in the Revolution. At the time of the Concordat, the First Consul rode to Notre-Dame in Louis XVI's carriage, with the martyred monarch's footman walking alongside. All this seemed to her to be symbolic. Napoleon's greatest crime, thundered Mme de Staël, and one for which all thinkers and writers will accuse him at the bar of humanity, was the establishment of a structure of despotism. There were special courts and military commissions to judge political crimes, 'that is to say, those which have most need of the constant protection of the law'. In addition, there was Fouché's five-fold organization of police spies: 'In modern times this political Inquisition has replaced the religious Inquisition'. Napoleon wanted his subjects to believe that he was everywhere present, and he always had plenty of zealous subordinates to carry out his despotic intentions to the letter in the smallest matters. He had 'the art of dazzling the masses' as well as the ability to corrupt individuals by offering them position, wealth and title. Above all, he was not only a man but a system: 'We must therefore examine him as a great problem whose solution is of importance for thought in all ages'. That was what she set out to do in her *Considerations*.

Mme de Staël could not help acknowledging, though, that Napoleon represented an extraordinary phenomenon in himself. 'Who could deny that Bonaparte was a man of transcendental genius in many respects?', she asked rhetorically. And she confessed how difficult it was for her to withstand his charisma: 'I have had . . . to resist the kind of perturbation that an extraordinary genius and an awesome destiny create in the imagination'. Moreover, she was bound to recognize that the Napoleonic Code of civil laws (much of which has endured in France) had its good points; that the imperial regime had contributed a good deal to art galleries (with paintings looted from conquered Europe, she might have added), to the beautification of Paris, to the construction of roads and canals. Under Napoleon, she allowed, there was considerable progress in the field of erudition and in that of the sciences, but only because these 'do not touch on politics'. Literature, in the broad sense she gave the term, could not flourish without free and open discussion, of the kind that had existed even under Louis XVI in the last years before the Revolution. One of her principal objections to the despot was his suppression of free inquiry and open debate.

It may be said that her recognition of any benefits that Napoleon might have brought to France, in the spheres where he continued the Revolution, was grudging; and was certainly far outweighed by her realization that he represented a dangerous precedent and that he had caused innumerable deaths in his ceaseless wars. It was not her place to make a case for the despot. Yet the various changing facets of Napoleon's career mean that he does present an ambivalent image whose complexity she was not prepared to admit. His armies did carry the ideas of the French Revolution with them into the countries they conquered. Paradoxically, Napoleon's conquests contributed to the birth of libertarian and national movements in Europe.

Nationalism was encouraged by Mme de Staël herself with her talk of 'national spirit' in *On Literature*, by which she meant the authentic character of each nation to be discovered and expressed in each country's literary works. Some of the great writers and poets in Europe in her day perceived what the author of *Corinne* had done to help this discovery. A great admirer of hers, the poet Pushkin, said she was 'the first to render full justice to the Russian people'. Another warm admirer, the poet Leopardi, was deeply stirred by her remarks on social and political life in Italy which were inspired by her desire to awaken the Italians to a better destiny. Goethe could do no less than acknowledge how she helped to enhance the image of Germany. It would be unfair to blame Mme de Staël for the course that nationalism in its exacerbated form was ultimately to take. For her, it signified national self-expression to balance individual self-expression, and the rejection of foreign oppression and occupation. It did not imply the kind of substitute religion that it was later to become.

Alongside her regard for the spirit of each nation, there was her feeling that each one had something important to offer the other, and to contribute to the idea of Europe as a whole. She saw herself as a European. Writing in the late 1790s, in a work that was never published in her lifetime, she spoke warmly of a union of writers and intellectuals that cut across frontiers: ' . . . in these days of hatred when men have rallied to different flags', she wrote, 'poets, scholars, philosophers, citizens of every nation and party, truly distinguished in some field of study, form a species of philosophical brotherhood . . .'. A few years later, at Coppet, where so many of the most cultivated figures of the age — including Constant, Schlegel, Sismondi — gathered around her and because of her, to meditate, to engage in discussion, to exchange ideas and furnish translations, there existed a sort of European civilization in miniature. Here were the liberal-minded members of the bourgeoisie as well as of the aristocracy, in a circle governed by respect for talent and independence. Here were Protestants and Catholics who participated in a dialogue uncommon at the time.

Mme de Staël encouraged these eminent spirits to write their important works — on drama, history, politics and religion — that stimulated the rise of the Romantic movement.

Finally, there remains something truly fine and moral, which ignorance and frivolity cannot enjoy: it is the association of all those who think, from one end of Europe to the other. Often they have no connection with each other; they are separated and scattered over great distances; but when they meet, a word is enough for recognition. It is not a particular religion, opinion or form of study, it is the cult of truth that unites them . . .

as she put it idealistically in *On Germany*. And she added: 'these are truly God's people, human beings who do not lose faith in the human race, and wish to preserve for it the empire of thought'. Here, Mme de Staël eloquently expressed her trust, founded in the Enlightenment, in an international cultural élite of the sort she herself had succeeded in fostering at Coppet, an élite of intellectuals who opposed first the authoritarianism of Napoleon and then the forces of reaction that predominated after his downfall.

What stands out above all today in Mme de Staël's career is her role as the leading intellectual opponent of the Napoleonic regime, as the great 'dissident' voice of the era, heard by all and esteemed by many of her peers. It is sometimes said by those with modern totalitarian regimes in mind that, by condemning Mme de Staël to exile (without trial), Napoleon did not treat her so very badly. In the context of the age, however, such arbitrary treatment of a woman of position whose sole instrument was her pen, was extremely harsh. Nor was she the only woman to be treated in this arbitrary manner: she was simply the most celebrated and made the most resounding protest.

Mme de Staël turned the very punishment Napoleon inflicted on her into a weapon against him. His persecution of her enabled her to see with greater clarity the implications of his despotic rule. With remarkable courage she carried her opposition in the name of truth and freedom to the furthest corners of Europe, pursuing him and exposing him in her writings. Thoroughly conscious of her challenging position, she was the first writer of outstanding repute in the nineteenth century to claim an active role for the intelligence and for literature itself in the struggle against the abuse of power.

The Destiny of Woman

Nothing could be further from the truth than the notion that Mme de Staël showed little interest in the condition of women. Inevitably, her entire experience was haunted by the contemporary ideal of femininity and by the conventional role allotted to women in her era. But throughout her life she was in revolt against the constrictions imposed on her sex. Benjamin Constant's remark has been much quoted: 'If she had known how to rule herself, she would have ruled the world . . .'. In reality, there was no way in which a woman of middle-class origin, whatever her self-control, could have ruled the world between 1766 and 1817. Simply through her talent Mme de Staël came nearest to doing so as a private individual and controversial writer, universally read and hugely influential.

There were, however, amid all her wide and varied concerns, certain areas that did not appear to interest her. Among these was the bid for equality made by Mary Wollstonecraft, or the demand for the rights of women presented by Olympe de Gouges. Since Germaine de Staël was eminently practical in outlook, she knew that claims of this sort — even during the Revolution when all seemed possible at first — were not likely to receive serious consideration, and even less likely to be met. After all, in her day — when the law still treated women as minors — participation in elections was something new in France for men. Besides, very few men fulfilled the requisite property condition to enable them to vote. The battle for universal suffrage (for men) still lay in the future.

The importance of Mme de Staël's contribution to an improvement in the status of women lay elsewhere, in her analysis of their present social predicament or what she called their 'situation in the social order'; her sharp criticism of this; and the part she played in stimulating an awareness of woman's fate and encouraging a change in mental outlook. No one before Mme de Staël had stressed so convincingly the vital importance of the general attitude to woman in each society in the development of its culture. The way in which women were viewed and treated was, for her, a token of the degree of civilization enjoyed at different periods of history. This is one of the principal themes of *On Literature*. There, she attributed to the influence of women the

107

very sensibility to be found in modern works, a new sensibility at once 'meditative and profound'. By emphasizing in her assessment of literature and society the role of her sex, Mme de Staël resolutely placed women on the cultural map. The high value allotted to womankind in the influential thought of the followers of the Utopian socialist comte de Saint-Simon and, indeed, in the wider movement of ideas up to the Revolution of 1848, doubtless owes something to Mme de Staël's views and egregious example.

The manner in which she revealed herself as a woman was also new. Jean-Jacques Rousseau had set the precedent for self-revelation, for the unveiling of weaknesses as well as virtues, in his *Confessions*, and here was a woman daring to follow in his footsteps, though necessarily with far more discretion. Contemporaries of hers were none the less amazed at the way she examined and analysed her innermost thoughts and feelings as a woman in *On the Influence of the Passions*. Stendhal, who thought this was her best book, despite his distaste for what he considered its turgid style, commented: 'She is a passionate spirit describing what she has felt'. According to Mme de Staël, love is rare, though all believe they have experienced it and know all about it. And she owned: 'There is an intimate conviction within oneself, that everything which follows love is nothingness, . . . and this conviction makes one think of death in the happiest moments of love'. Such candour, however muted in modern eyes, on the subject of female sexuality, was not the tone then expected of a woman writer.

Woman's 'deplorable' fate — that was a subject to which she constantly returned. Youthful illusion, and then, at twenty-five, 'at the exact moment when life ceases to grow', a cruel change occurs: 'in many respects your fate is sealed, and men consider carefully whether it suits them to bind their fate to yours . . .', she brooded in her late twenties. By the time she came to write the second preface to her youthful essay on Rousseau, in 1814, at the age of forty-eight, she declared that 'Everything moves towards decline in woman's fate, except thought.' She was convinced of the view, commonly held in her day (and later), that a woman's life was finished at thirty, and she looked to serious study for consolation in the years that remained.

The decent education of women was therefore of great importance to her. This subject was then regarded as part of woman's proper sphere'. She saw the act of thinking and the acquisition of knowledge as an enrichment, a source of private content. Women of the leisure class in particular, so inclined to frivolity and to an obsessional concern with social niceties, were admonished: 'If you do not breathe higher air, you are nothing but a well-taught doll.' Women should be encouraged to cultivate their minds, she wrote in *On Literature*, foreseeing a time when legislators would pay serious attention to the education of women, and would enact laws to protect them.

Mme de Staël attacked the general failure to develop women's faculties like those of men, to grant them equal education: 'To enlighten, educate, improve women like men . . . that is the best secret for accomplishing all reasonable aims, for all social and political relations which it is desirable to establish on a lasting foundation'. Such equal education, she hoped, would lead to an admirable 'communication of minds' in marriage. Of course, it was possible, she granted, that by developing women's power of reason, they would become enlightened about 'the ills inseparable from their fate; but the same argument would be applicable to the result of enlightenment in general concerning the happiness of humankind . . .'. In short, enlightenment was bound to make people understand the hard realities of their position and would prompt them to seek some remedy.

One must work for an improvement in women's fate, she urged. Women should no longer be confined automatically to 'domestic cares' or trivial pursuits, if these did not suit them. In line with her belief (after Rousseau) in the importance of each individual's authentic development, she asked with Corinne: 'Should not each woman, like each man, clear a path for herself in accordance with her character and gifts?' Equally potent was the question, printed in italics, in *Corinne*: '*Is there any harm in knowing Greek, in earning one's livelihood by one's work?*' When one recalls how long it took to open higher institutions of learning to women, and even longer to render their gainful employment socially respectable, one realizes how revolutionary Mme de Staël's standpoint was in the eyes of her public, and especially her women readers.

Another matter entirely was the role of women in politics, in that era definitely not 'their proper sphere'. Doubtless thinking of her association with Narbonne, she admitted that 'men do not see any sort of general usefulness in encouraging the success of women in this career'. Even less do men want women as rivals, she averred. The rare women who are the exception to the rule (like herself) arouse jealousy and hatred. 'Man derives satisfaction from the superiority of his nature and, like Pygmalion, he prostrates himself only in the presence of the labour of his own hands', she declared with no little irony.

As for women, in her experience most of them proved hostile to the exceptional female out of rivalry, stupidity or on principle. (Stendhal confirmed this when he told his sister Pauline that women were envious of Mme de Staël's candour, and that he had actually seen a woman consumed by jealousy on reading *Delphine*.) To attain to *gloire*, women have to sacrifice personal happiness and a quiet mind, owned Germaine. Her general advice, in the study of the passions, would seem to be that women should not seek a career in politics or literature unless they were prepared to pay as high a price as she felt she had herself.

On the whole, Mme de Staël was not primarily concerned with those women who were content with their lot or who resigned themselves to it. She was preoccupied with herself, with rare beings of a similar nature, with what she called 'the superior woman', 'the exceptional woman', the talented woman. No doubt she overlooked the vast majority. No doubt, too, she was condescending and (perhaps understandably) vain in perceiving the distance between herself and most of the rest of her sex in her day, including many of the lesser women writers.

Exceptional women, she knew, were unjustly treated, for society was armed against any woman who wished to enjoy the same kind of reputation as that of men, she declared. A man of genius, once he became powerful, would have to be treated with a degree of consideration denied to the gifted woman. Above all, he could refute calumny without loss of reputation. This a woman could not do, as Mme de Staël discovered in her own case, because any attempt at self-justification on her part merely added to her notoriety. 'Is she not an extraordinary woman? That says everything; she is left to her own resources . . . . She leads a singular existence, like the pariahs of India . . . an object of curiosity, perhaps of envy, and really deserving only pity.' This self-pitying apologia of hers in *On Literature* did not pass without arousing the wit of hostile critics.

Mme de Staël's response to such criticism would be obliquely expressed in the creation of *Corinne*. Here was the great consoling fantasy of the woman artist of genius, endowed with all the talents, an object of universal admiration, respect and love. Yet Corinne is not just the first woman of genius to be the heroine of a novel, she is also the first woman in fiction to lead a totally independent life in an Italy so enamoured of art and beauty that the freedom of her life-style arouses no adverse comment among the Italians. It is discreetly conveyed that Corinne has had several lovers before Oswald arrives on the scene, although she is in love for the first time with him. This independence, combined with artistic brilliance, offered contemporaries a heady brew. At first, the reader sees only Corinne's fame and freedom. It is only as a consequence of her love for Oswald, and his failure to measure up to her ideal conception of him, that Corinne loses both her gifts and her liberty, and declines into suffering and death.

The influence of *Corinne* on women writers in the nineteenth century should not be underestimated. That influence was doubtless psychological rather than strictly literary. Like so much of Mme de Staël's writing in different fields, this novel raised the morale of a depressed section of humanity hitherto only dimly aware of its own strengths, merits and potential. It was the example of Corinne, the woman artist of genius, determined to be true to herself and her talents, that encouraged and inspired women writers from Elizabeth Barrett Browning to George Eliot, and from Harriet Beecher Stowe to Margaret Fuller (the 'Yankee Corinna'). The independent life-style of Corinne, too, made a deep impression on some, until it was overshadowed by the more startlingly dramatic role-model offered by the conduct of George Sand in the 1830s.

Mme de Staël's numerous liaisons did not prevent her from keeping in view an ideal of marriage. She was even ready to admit (in fortunately pre-Freudian innocence) that, had she only been born sooner, and consequently had she been able to marry Necker, she too could have enjoyed a lasting union in constancy! She wrote in *Corinne*: 'how happy are those women whom the sacred bond of matrimony has led gently from love to friendship . . . !' While she was staying at Juniper Hall with Narbonne, she had been deeply moved by a devoted English husband and wife (Mr and Mrs Locke), and she alluded to them in her study of the passions, commenting on the rarity of such married bliss. In *Delphine*, M. de Belmont and his wife embody an ideal marriage. Delphine herself asserts that 'the destiny of a woman is finished when she has not married the man she loves . . .'; and she speaks of 'the supreme good, love in marriage'. Sainte-Beuve thought Mme de Staël was haunted by this ideal.

However, if woman's role were destined to lie in conjugal devotion, she wrote in *On Germany*, then the wife's reward should be the husband's 'scrupulous fidelity'. According to religion, there was no distinction between the duties of husband and wife in this regard, whereas society permitted (and would continue to permit) the injustice of the double standard. She objected to what she called paradoxically 'the tyrannical freedom' which men had allocated to themselves. They could do as they pleased, whereas a woman would suffer humiliation and would lose her good name. What she wanted was joint responsibility rather than joint licence. 'As long as there is not some revolution in ideas that changes men's view of the constancy imposed on them by the bond of marriage, there will always be a war between the sexes, a war that is secret, everlasting, cunning, treacherous. . . .' It was therefore a revolution in consciousness that she wished to bring about in the relations between men and women. Here, she was in advance of her time.

Far-seeing and intrepid as she was in some respects, Mme de Staël could be timid on the subject of femininity. It would seem that she feared as well as resented any imputation that she might not be perfectly 'feminine' in the current understanding of the term in her own day, when the intellectual faculty was assigned to men alone. Modest womanly devotion as daughter, wife and mother; womanly weakness in constant need of masculine protection and support — these formed an essential part of the feminine ideal in which she believed (or thought she believed) quite as much as did the majority of the women of the age. Nothing served so well to keep women in their subordinate place as this concept of what was truly womanly. This ideal did not harmonize with her qualities of courage and independence, her aspirations to *gloire* and, above all, her conduct throughout her life.

The conflict within Mme de Staël herself is powerfully symbolized in *Corinne*, where the timid, modest, rather shadowy Lucile is said to resemble a soft and gentle Madonna by Correggio, while her brilliant half-sister is compared with Domenichino's ardent, almost speaking Sibyl. The dying Corinne advises Lucile somewhat domineeringly: 'You must be both yourself and myself at the same time'. But such a conjunction of contrary ideals seems scarcely possible. In fact, the reconciliation between these contraries in the novel is largely illusory. Corinne dominates Lucile, instructing her and virtually using her to work her posthumous revenge, for in moulding Lucile in her own image she wants Oswald to be endlessly reminded of herself after her death. The Sibyl may lose in the worldly sense, but she preserves her immortal power over the minds of men.

Reputation

The reputation of Mme de Staël was at its height at the time of her death in 1817, and immediately after. The posthumous publication of *Ten Years of Exile* and the *Considerations*, together with the edition of her complete works in 1820–1 (supervised by her son Auguste), kept her name before the public. Mme de Staël's family and friends were, however, most anxious to suppress certain aspects of her writings that might give offence to people who were still living, or that might interfere with her son-in-law's political career. They sweetened, softened or expurgated her text.

Some idea of the extent of her reputation during her lifetime in the early years of the nineteenth century can be gleaned from the letters and diaries of Henri Beyle. The future author of *The Charterhouse of Parma* read Mme de Staël's books with care, sometimes re-reading them a year or two later, revising his opinion and viewing them with greater comprehension or favour. He recommended her works (with reservations) to his sister Pauline as well. Moreover, Stendhal found Mme de Staël's thoughts sufficiently useful to extract passages and 'translate them into French', as he put it, that is, into his own highly succinct style. From *Delphine*, he derived 'many ingenious and even profound ideas on Parisian society'. A number of the ideas he made his own — on the nature of the quest for happiness, for instance; on French fear of ridicule and the absence of vanity in the Italian character; on the significance of Shakespeare as compared with Racine; on the need for literature to be 'Romantic' or modern in order to express a changed and changing experience — he found in Mme de Staël's writings. The *Considerations*, however, with their severe judgement of the emperor, raised the hackles of this former Napoleonic functionary, and prompted him to return to his life of Napoleon, which he never completed.

In the year after Mme de Staël's death, Stendhal suggested that her reputation might well not extend much beyond 1860. Like other prophecies of his (including the one concerning the date when he himself would be valued at his true worth) it had an element of truth. In France, it was chiefly the leaders of the generation that came to the fore in the 1820s who paid her hommage. In his youth, that subtle and influential critic, Sainte-Beuve, rarely generous with his praise, came under her spell. The young Victor Hugo, in 1824, called Mme de Staël 'a woman of genius who was the first to utter the words "Romantic literature" in France'. Three years later, he even declared that she had already said what he was trying to say about the new French drama, of which he was the principal theorist and practician.

In the 1830s, though, whatever inspiration George Sand may have drawn from her predecessor's works and example, with which she was well acquainted, she did not warm to Mme de Staël. Once, she unkindly called the creator of *Corinne* 'this man-woman', voicing the kind of accusation that was often levelled against herself. She was deliberately provocative about her celebrated forerunner. Apparently, George Sand thought the author of *On Literature* not only more fortunate than herself, but also more of an intellectual. Sainte-Beuve complained about this attitude: while calling George Sand the most important woman in literature since Mme de Staël, he insisted on the younger writer's debt to her predecessor. It was George Sand's humanitarian Utopian socialism that would supersede the liberalism of Mme de Staël. Still, there were some forty editions of *Corinne* between 1807 and 1872, by which time both writers had yielded place to the advocates of a more practical feminist policy.

Inevitably, Mme de Staël's reputation varied, as it did in her lifetime, according to the political stance of her critics. Favoured, in the nineteenth century and after, by liberals or liberal sympathizers, she was loathed by all those who saw her as a leading product and exponent of the Enlightenment and of the French Revolution, which they considered to be its disastrous outcome. In addition to bitter opponents of the Revolution and all its works, there would be those writers in reaction against the Romantic movement as a whole with which she became associated. Nor was there ever any lack of prejudiced critics who resented her simply as an imperfect woman grotesquely involved in political and other matters that were long deemed a masculine preserve.

What is Mme de Staël's legacy? Certainly, her name is to be found in any serious account of the literature and ideas as well as the history of the revolutionary and post-revolutionary period in Europe. Sometimes, one comes across a strikingly generous appreciation of her contribution. For instance, Ian Watt, in his notable work, *The Rise of the Novel: Studies in Defoe, Richardson and Fielding*, published in 1957, acknowledged his debt to her, remarking that 'the first important study of the novel in its larger background [Mme de Staël's *On Literature Considered in its Relations with Social Institutions*] anticipated many of the elements' of his own book. Indeed, it is during the last thirty years or so that there has been a great revival of interest in Mme de Staël. Not only biographies, but also studies of her works as a whole have appeared, together with examinations of her novels and of innumerable aspects of her thought and temperament. Recent years have seen modern scholarly editions of some of her most important books, together with the first publication of her travel diaries. Her correspondence, too, is being collected and edited in its entirety for the first time.

It is perhaps less as an artist than as a questing intellectual that Mme de Staël survives today. She was not strictly an original thinker: rather was she one who formulates and popularizes notions and aspirations that are in the air. This is a task which requires highly sensitive antennae, responsive to the slightest hint of variation in concepts and sensibility; and she knew how to give expression to these subtle trends and their likely consequences in a manner that could be readily understood and assimilated.

Of the rivers of words that she committed to paper, much has been absorbed into the ocean of widely accepted ideas about literature and politics. Yet there remains a good deal in her writing that is still of vital importance today, in an era of increasing violence, fanaticism and barbarism. Her impassioned yet eminently reasonable voice reminds each reader to consider the opponent as a human being. She herself was always ready to help people who did not share her views, whether they were aristocrats persecuted under the Jacobin regime and the Directory, or later, Bonapartists threatened under Louis XVIII. For her, friendship was supreme, and it implied devoted assistance, even at personal risk to herself.

It might be said that, like many liberal advocates of reason and tolerance, she tended to overestimate the merits of enlightenment as a panacea for all ills, and to underestimate the extent of sheer human perversity. In the beginning, malice took her by surprise; but soon, harsh experience of the world revealed to her the power of wickedness. She stood resolutely with those who, despite evil, refuse to despair of human nature. Her writings, constructed to cover the void she sensed beneath human existence, insist on hopefulness, and have been called by one of her most perceptive critics, Simone Balayé, 'the work of hope of a deeply despairing spirit'.

Emotionally theatrical, yet cerebral in her quest for understanding; egotistical and self-indulgent, yet compassionate and thoughtful in her conduct to many; deeply melancholy and full of life and gaiety; quixotic and practical; careful and audacious — here was a creature of startling contradictions. Above all, she had integrity, for she could have purchased a quiet existence at home with a show of outward conformity and with a few words of flattery addressed to Napoleon. The author of *Corinne* was the first woman of middle-class birth to stun the world with her great talent, to imprint it upon both the literary and the political spheres, and to employ it to alter the mentality of women as well as men.

Not so very long ago, it used to be the fashion to speak of Mme de Staël in a tone of amused condescension that would scarcely be acceptable today. Those who seek to uphold the value of the individual in the face of an ever-increasing threat to freedom from the forces of perverse ideology, materialist philosophy, or the encroachments of state power, will always have good reason to return to her. For she stands as a great fighter in the never-ending battle to increase human potential and to procure and preserve the essential liberties.

116

Chronology

1732	Birth of Jacques Necker, Geneva.
1737	Birth of Suzanne Curchod, Crassier (Vaud).
1764	Marriage of Jacques Necker and Suzanne Curchod, Paris.
1766	22 April. Birth of Anne Louise Germaine Necker, Paris.
1774	Louis XVI ascends the French throne.
1775	Birth of Jane Austen.
1776	The Neckers visit England with their daughter.
1777	Necker appointed Directeur-Général des Finances.
1778	M. de Staël, Swedish attaché in Paris, seeks the hand of Mlle Necker, aged twelve, in marriage. Mlle Necker and her mother visit Voltaire. Illness and convalescence of Mlle Necker at Saint-Ouen. She writes a comedy, *The Inconveniences of Parisian Life*
1781	Louis XVI asks Necker to resign.
1784	Necker buys the château of Coppet, near Geneva.
1784–5	The Neckers visit southern France.
1785	Mlle Necker keeps a diary.
1785–6	She writes stories, including *Histoire de Pauline, Mirza.*
1786	6 January. Her marriage contract signed by the royal family at Versailles. 14 January. Marriage of Mlle Necker and M. de Staël solemnized at the Swedish Embassy, rue du Bac, Paris. 31 January. Mme de Staël presented at the French

court.

She begins sending a newsletter to King Gustavus III of Sweden; writes a play, *Sophie, or the Secret Feelings*, and begins work on her *Letters on the Writings and Character of Jean-Jacques Rousseau*.

1787   Louis XVI exiles Necker.
22 July. Birth of Gustavine, goddaughter of the king and queen of Sweden.
She writes a play, *Jane Gray*.

1788   Necker recalled.
Affair with Talleyrand. She meets comte Louis de Narbonne: their liaison.
Limited publication of her *Letters on the Writings and Character of Jean-Jacques Rousseau*.

1789   7 April. Death of Gustavine.
4 May. Mme de Staël witnesses the procession for the opening of the States General.
5 May. She is present at the opening session of the States General.
11 July. Necker is again sent into exile. A few days later, he is recalled, and returns to Paris from Basle in triumph.
14 July. Fall of the Bastille.
5–6 October. Mme de Staël sees the riots at Versailles and the forced return of the royal family to Paris.

1790   19 June. Her friend, Mathieu de Montmorency, proposes the abolition of titles of nobility in the Assembly.
14 July. She is present at the Fête de la Fédération, first anniversary of the Revolution.
She writes her *Eulogy of M. de Guibert*.
3 August. Birth of Auguste, her son by Narbonne.
3 September. Necker resigns.
October. Limited publication of *Sophie* and *Jane Gray*.

1791   January to May. Her salon is a meeting-place for

the moderates, including Sieyès, and much of the new Constitution is formulated there.

16 April. She publishes an unsigned article in *Les Indépendants*.

21 June. Flight of Louis XVI and the royal family: their capture at Varennes.

3 September. Constitution of 1791.

6 December. Narbonne, whose career she has sought to advance, becomes Minister of War.

1792   9 March. Narbonne falls.

16 March. Assassination of King Gustavus III of Sweden (plot of Count Ribbing and others).

July. She and Narbonne suggest a new plan of escape for Louis XVI: it is rejected by Marie-Antoinette.

10 August. Proclamation of the First Republic. She rescues several of her endangered aristocratic friends.

2 September. She is nearly massacred as she tries to leave Paris. She is brought before Robespierre.

3 September. She is allowed to leave for Switzerland.

20 November. Birth of Albert, her second son by Narbonne.

End December. She leaves for England.

1793   20 January–25 May. At Juniper Hall in Surrey, where she supports Narbonne, Montmorency and others. She meets Fanny Burney, visits London, and works on her study *On the Influence of the Passions upon the Happiness of Individuals and of Nations*.

21 January. Execution of Louis XVI.

25 May. She takes leave of Narbonne at Dover.

31 May. Fall of the Girondins. Inauguration of the Reign of Terror.

June to September. At Coppet. She meets Count Adolph Ribbing in exile.

5 October. The new republican calendar (brumaire, prairial, etc.)

October. The trial and execution of Marie-Antoinette.

Mme de Staël hides some of her endangered aristocratic friends in Switzerland. She publishes *Thoughts on the Queen's Trial*.

1794
Publishes her story, *Zulma*.
April. Travels with Ribbing.
She rescues several friends under threat of execution.
15 May. Death of Mme Necker.
June/July. Apogee of the Reign of Terror.
27 July 1794 (9 Thermidor). Fall of Robespierre. End of the Reign of Terror.
End July. Arrival of Narbonne in Switzerland: end of their liaison.
18 September. She meets Benjamin Constant.
First edition of her *Reflections on Peace* published in Switzerland.

1795
Benjamin Constant resides at her home.
Spring. She publishes her *Essay on Fiction*.
23 April. Sweden is the first country to recognize the new French government: M. de Staël received at the National Convention.
25 May. Mme de Staël arrives in Paris with Benjamin Constant and opens her salon in the midst of working-class riots.
3 June. She declares her faith in the Republic.
Summer. She completes her *Reflections on Internal Peace*.
18 August. Legendre accuses of her of conspiracy in the National Convention.
Beginning September. She leaves Paris.
5 October (13 Vendémiaire). Abortive royalist *coup d'état*. She is compromised because she helps proscribed aristocrats.
15 October. She is exiled by the Committee of Public Safety: the decree is rescinded.
27 October. The Directory in power.
December. She leaves for Switzerland with Benjamin Constant. She finishes her study of the passions.

Winter 1795/6. Conspiracy of Equals led by 'Grac-chus' Babeuf.

1796   22 April. She is to be arrested if she returns to Paris.
        Autumn. She publishes *On the Influence of the Passions*.
        End December. She is allowed to return to Paris.

1797   January to May. She stays with Benjamin Con-stant at his estate.
        8 June. Birth of Albertine.
        Summer. The Club de Salm is founded by Mme de Staël, Benjamin Constant and other moderates. Revision of the Constitution of Year III.
        16 July. Talleyrand, whose return to France she has engineered, is appointed Minister of Foreign Affairs with her help.
        4 September (18 Fructidor). Mme de Staël sup-ports the *coup d'état* but disapproves of the ensuing repression. She saves some of her friends.
        5 September (19 Fructidor). Law requires oath of hatred to royalty.
        6 December. She meets General Napoleon Bona-parte for the first time.

1798   January. She returns to Switzerland. French army invades Canton of Vaud.
        She writes *Concerning the Present Circumstances for Ending the French Revolution* which she does not publish. She begins *On Literature Considered in its Relations with Social Institutions*.

1799   July. Expelled by the Directory.
        9 November (18 Brumaire). She arrives in Paris on the evening of Bonaparte's *coup d'état*.
        Autumn. She meets Mme Récamier for the first time.
        December. Bonaparte is First Consul. Benjamin Constant is nominated to the Tribunate by Sieyès.

1800   5 January. Benjamin Constant's speech in the Tri-bunate annoys Bonaparte.

April. She publishes *On Literature* — attacked in the press.
June. Napoleon's victory at Marengo.
Summer. She begins *Delphine*.
November. Second edition of *On Literature*.
Separation from M. de Staël.

1801	At Coppet, she meets Sismondi. November. She returns to Paris.
1802	17 January. Bonaparte dismisses the moderate members of the Tribunate, including Benjamin Constant. March. Peace of Amiens. April. Ceremonies to celebrate the Concordat. Conspiracy of General Moreau. May. Bonaparte is Consul for Life. Death of M. de Staël. December. She publishes *Delphine*. Bonaparte forbids her to stay in Paris.
1803	May. Renewal of war with Great Britain. September. She arrives at Maffliers. October. She is ordered to keep forty leagues from Paris. 25 October. She leaves for Germany with Benjamin Constant. 13 November. She stays in Frankfurt. 14 December. She arrives in Weimar. She is received at court, and meets Wieland, Schiller, Goethe.
1804	March. Promulgation of Napoleon's Civil Code. She leaves Weimar with Benjamin Constant. At Leipzig, they exchange a written promise to marry. He returns to Switzerland. *ca* 8 March. She arrives in Berlin, is fêted at Court and in the salons, and engages A.W. Schlegel as tutor to her children. 9 April. Death of Necker. 18 April. She leaves Berlin, believing her father to be ill. 22 April. Benjamin Constant rejoins her at Weimar and informs her of her father's death.

May. Proclamation of the Empire.

19 May. She arrives at Coppet.

Summer. She decides against marriage with Benjamin Constant.

Autumn. She publishes *Manuscripts of M. Necker* with her essay *On the Character of M. Necker and his Private Life*.

2 December. Napoleon crowned Emperor.

11 December. She leaves for Italy with A.W. Schlegel. Sismondi joins them later.

29 December. She meets the poet Vincenzo Monti in Milan.

805

4 February. She arrives in Rome.

17 February. She leaves for Naples.

Mid March. She returns to Rome, frequents Roman society, meets the young Portuguese diplomat Pedro de Souza.

May. She travels through Florence and Venice to Milan, where she arrives after Napoleon is crowned king of Italy.

15 June. She leaves Milan for Coppet.

Summer. The gathering of writers and scholars at Coppet. She meets Prosper de Barante and begins a five-year liaison with him. She starts work on *Corinne, or Italy*.

Winter. She writes a play, *Hagar in the Desert*.

2 December. Napoleon victorious at Austerlitz.

806

April. She stays near Auxerre.

September. She resides at Rouen.

November. She stays near Meulan, finishing *Corinne, or Italy*.

807

April. She spends a few days in secret in Paris.

1 May. She publishes *Corinne* — an immense success.

25 June. Napoleon and Tsar Alexander I meet on the raft at Tilsit.

4 December. She leaves for Vienna with A.W. Schlegel.

28 December. In an audience with the Emperor at Chambéry, young Auguste fails to obtain a pardon for his mother.

| 1808 | Winter in Vienna. Affair with Count Maurice O'Donnell. |

1808 — Winter in Vienna. Affair with Count Maurice O'Donnell.
31 March. A.W. Schlegel begins to deliver his lectures on drama.
May. Joseph Bonaparte becomes king of Spain.
5 June. Benjamin Constant secretly marries Charlotte von Hardenberg.
Summer. Mme de Staël begins work on *On Germany*.
December. Napoleon invades Spain.

1809 — 9 May. Charlotte informs Mme de Staël that she is Constant's wife. The couple are persuaded to keep the marriage secret and Constant follows Mme de Staël to Coppet.

1810 — Censorship reinforced in February.
April. She resides at the château de Chaumont.
Nicolle begins to set *On Germany* in print.
Napoleon marries Marie-Louise of Austria.
3 June. Fouché replaced by Savary, duc de Rovigo, as Minister of Police.
August. She resides at the château de Fossé.
24 September. Rovigo orders her to leave within 24 hours and to deliver to him the manuscripts and proofs of *On Germany*.
6 October. She leaves for Coppet.
14/15 October. *On Germany* is pulped.
November. In Geneva she meets young John Rocca who courts her.

1811 — February. She is harassed by the new *préfet*.
May. She and Rocca exchange a promise to marry in the presence of a Protestant pastor.
August. Mathieu de Montmorency visits her and is sent into exile.
September. Mme Récamier visits her and is exiled.

Summer. She meets the Duke of Wellington.
September. Congress of Vienna.

1815   1 March. Napoleon returns from Elba.
10 March. She leaves Paris for Coppet.
20 March. Napoleon enters Paris.
18 June. Napoleon is defeated at Waterloo.
22 June. He abdicates for the second time.
July. Restoration of Louis XVIII followed by the
White Terror (royalist atrocities in southern France).
September. She vows allegiance to Louis XVIII
and is received at court. Albertine is betrothed to
Victor, duc de Broglie. They leave with Mme de
Staël, Rocca and A.W. Schlegel for Italy.

1816   January. In Milan she publishes *On the Spirit of
Translations*, and winters in Pisa.
20 February. Marriage of Albertine and the duc de
Broglie in Pisa.
Summer. She welcomes Byron at Coppet.
10 October. She marries John Rocca secretly at
Coppet.
16 October. They leave for Paris.

1817   21 February. She suffers a stroke.
14 July. Death of Mme de Staël in Paris.
18 July. Death of Jane Austen.
28 July. Mme de Staël is buried in the family
mausoleum at Coppet.

1818   30 January. Death of John Rocca.
Publication of *Considerations on the Principal Events of
the French Revolution*.
November. Allied occupation of France ends.

1820   Publication of *Ten Years of Exile* and of *Complete
Works*.

Select Bibliography

Works of Mme de Staël

Oeuvres Complètes, 17 vols., 1820–1

MODERN EDITIONS

De l'Allemagne, ed. J. de Pange & S. Balayé, 1958–60.

Les Carnets de Voyage de Mme de Staël, ed. S. Balayé, 1971.

Des Circonstances actuelles qui peuvent terminer la révolution et des principes qui doivent fonder la république en France, ed. L. Omacini, 1979.

Dix années d'exil, Introduction by S. Balayé, 1966.

De la Littérature considérée dans ses rapports avec les institutions sociales, ed. P. Van Tieghem, 2 vols., 1959.

CORRESPONDENCE

Correspondance générale, ed. B. Jasinski, 1962 — in progress

Lettres de Mme de Staël à Benjamin Constant, ed. Mme de Nolde, 1928

Lettres de Mme de Staël à Narbonne, ed. G. Solovieff, 1960

Lettres de Mme de Staël à Juliette Récamier, ed. E. Beau de

Loménie, 1952

Lettres de Mme de Staël à Ribbing, ed. S. Balayé, 1960

Lettres de Mme de Staël à Pedro de Souza, ed. B. d'Andlau, 1979

Miscellaneous Studies on Mme de Staël

Cahiers staëliens, published by the Société d'études staëliennes

Mme de Staël et l'Europe, Colloque de Coppet (1966) 1970

Le Groupe de Coppet, Colloque de Coppet (1974) 1977

General Works Concerning Mme de Staël

Andlau, B. d', *La Jeunesse de Mme de Staël*, 1970

Balayé, S., *Mme de Staël. Lumières et Liberté*, 1979

Bénichou, P., *Le Sacre de l'écrivain*, 1973

Beyle, H., *see* Stendhal

Blennerhasset, Lady, *Mme de Staël et son temps*, 3 vols., 1890

Blessington, Lady, *Conversations of Lord Byron*, ed. E. J. Lovell, 1969

Burney, F., *Journals and Letters*, ed. J. Hemslow & A. Douglas, vol. 2, 1972

Byron, Lord, *Letters and Journals*, ed. Leslie A. Marchand, vol. 3, *1813–14*, 1974; vol. 5, *1816–17*, 1976

Chateaubriand, F.-R. de, *Mémoires d'outre-tombe*, ed. M. Levaillant, 4 vols., 1948

Constant, B., *Oeuvres*, ed. A. Roulin, 1957

Diesbach, G. de, *Mme de Staël*, 1983

Gautier, P., *Mme de Staël et Napoléon*, 1903

Geyl, P., *Napoleon, For and Against*, 1949

Guillemin, H., *Mme de Staël, Benjamin Constant et Napoléon*, 1959

Gutwirth, M., *Mme de Staël, Novelist*, 1978

Gwynne, G. E., *Mme de Staël et la Révolution française*, 1969

Herold, J. C., *Mistress to an Age: A Life of Mme de Staël*, 1958

Larg, D. G., *Mme de Staël: la vie dans l'oeuvre 1766–1800*, 1924

—, *Mme de Staël: la seconde vie 1800–1807*, 1928

Litto, V. del, *La Vie intellectuelle de Stendhal 1802–1821*, 1959

Luppé, R. de, *Les idées littéraires de Mme de Staël et l'héritage des lumières 1795–1800*, 1969

Mistler, J., *Mme de Staël et Maurice O'Donnell*, 1926

Moers, E., *Literary Women*, 1976

Necker de Saussure, A., *Notice sur le caractère et les écrits de Mme de Staël* (in Mme de Staël, *Oeuvres complètes*, vol. I)

Pange, V. de, *Mme de Staël et le duc de Wellington*, 1962

—, *Le plus beau de toutes les fêtes*, 1980

Sainte-Beuve, C.-A., *Oeuvres*, ed. M. Leroy, 2 vols., 1956, 1960

Stendhal, *Correspondance*, ed. H. Martineau & V. del Litto, 3 vols., 1968

—, *Oeuvres intimes*, ed. H. Martineau, 1955

Index